How to Conduct Organizational Surveys

How to Conduct Organizational Surveys

A Step-by-Step Guide

Jack E. Edwards
Marie D. Thomas
Paul Rosenfeld
Stephanie Booth-Kewley

SAGE Publications
International Educational and Professional Publisher
Thousand Oaks   London   New Delhi

For information address:

SAGE Publications, Inc.
2455 Teller Road
Thousand Oaks, California 91320
E-mail: order@sagepub.com

SAGE Publications Ltd.
6 Bonhill Street
London EC2A 4PU
United Kingdom

SAGE Publications India Pvt. Ltd.
M-32 Market
Greater Kailash I
New Delhi 110 048 India

Printed in the United States of America

Library of Congress Cataloging-in-Publication Data

Main entry under title:

How to conduct organizational surveys : a step-by-step guide /
        authors, Jack E. Edwards . . . [et al.].
                p.   cm.
        Includes bibliographical references and index.
        ISBN 0-8039-5512-X (cloth : acid-free paper). — ISBN
0-8039-5513-8 (pbk. : acid-free paper)
            1. Employee attitude surveys—Methodology.   I. Edwards, Jack E.
HF5549.5.A83H69   1996
658.3'14'0723—dc20   96-35628
                                                                                          CIP

This book is printed on acid-free paper.

97 98 99 00 01 10 9 8 7 6 5 4 3 2

Acquiring Editor:	Harry Briggs
Editorial Assistant:	Frances Borghi
Production Editor:	Sherrise Purdum
Production Assistant:	Karen Wiley
Typesetter/Designer:	Christina Hill
Cover Designer:	Lesa Valdez
Print Buyer:	Anna Chin

Contents

Preface

A manufacturing company is downsizing and wants to know the effect of the downsizing on employee morale. A computer corporation is considering moving its headquarters and needs to determine how many employees it would need to relocate. A multinational consulting firm has had a rash of sexual harassment complaints and seeks to determine the extent of the problem. An automobile company is planning to redesign its line of sports cars and wishes to see how its loyal customers will react to the changes.

To answer these and many other business-related questions, organizations are increasingly turning to surveys. Developing expertise in the organizational survey process is by no means an easy task. It is a process that can reap great benefits if the steps are correctly executed, but it can cause harm if done improperly.

Although conducting an organizational survey can be a difficult, expensive, and labor-intensive effort, it also has its rewards. Survey designers have the satisfaction of seeing a need for information turn into items; these items elicit data that, in turn, provide answers to the original questions (Rosenfeld, Edwards, & Thomas, 1993). For management, surveys can suggest ways to increase productivity, improve morale, and reduce costs. Through organizational surveys, employees can communicate their concerns and questions to management. Surveys can also provide a vehicle for employees to participate in the company's decision-making process and involve them in solving problems rather than simply griping or suffering in silence (Carney, 1994; Salemme, 1995).

We have written this book as a resource for conducting surveys within organizational settings. It is designed to provide those who desire to conduct organizational surveys with step-by-step, how-to instructions. In the chapters that follow, we describe the issues that must be addressed at each step in the survey process, the advantages and disadvantages that result from many of the choices that must be made, and practical lessons that we have learned (often, the hard way). This book should be a useful and practical tool even for people with little or no experience with the survey process. Moreover, we have attempted to identify sound survey practices in other professions (e.g., marketing and public opinion research) that generalize to organizational surveys.

We intend this book to be an easy-to-understand guide to the technical and practical considerations that arise when conducting surveys in real-world organizational settings. In particular, our book is written for the manager who has little experience conducting an in-house survey or contracting external survey consultants. Similarly, our book should be a useful introduction to graduate students (e.g., in business and industrial-organizational psychology) who must make the transition from theory to practice. Toward this end, we address most common survey issues with both references to the survey research literature and real-life examples. Although a book this size cannot address every issue in depth, we provide citations to survey literature that we have found helpful.

We are indebted to a number of people for their professional and personal support. At Sage, we will always be grateful to Harry Briggs for his faith in our abilities and his patience with the pace of our productivity. Comments from two anonymous reviewers helped us focus an earlier draft of the book and identify areas of improvement. Some of the comments were so articulate that we included them with little modification.

We also benefited greatly from the continued support of many current and former colleagues and friends. Thanks to David Alderton, Dan Landis, Nambury Raju, Larry Waters, Paul Crawford, Catherine Riordan, Bob Giacalone, Zannette Perry, Steve Knouce, Amy Culbertson, John Sheposh, Mike White, Aileen Conroy, John Kantor, Patricia Thomas, Edmund Thomas, Carol Newell, Kristin David, Sharon Le, Richard Sorenson, George Edward Seymour, Tim Elig, Anita Lancaster, and, of course, Walt Peterson. On a personal level, we would like to thank Deborah McCormick, Mary Edwards, Harold Edwards, Susie Hoke, Patti Groves, Jerry Larson, Edward Thomas, Fred Thomas, Barbara Rooney, Abraham and Judes Rosenfeld, the Shanskes, Mary Sellen, Brian Kewley, Andrew Kewley, Norman and Joyce Booth, and Donna Booth for their continued love, support, and encouragement.

Organizational Surveys
An Overview

1

A survey is a way of obtaining self-reported information about the attitudes, beliefs, opinions, behaviors, or other characteristics of a population (Babbie, 1973; Rosenfeld, Edwards, & Thomas, 1995). More formally, Rossi, Wright, and Anderson (1983) state that surveys "consist of relatively systematic, standardized approaches to the collection of information on individuals, households, or larger organized entities, through the questioning of systematically identified samples of individuals" (p. 1). From these definitions, we see that the term *survey* refers to both the instrument used to gather data and the processes employed when using the instrument.

Although the focus of this book is on using surveys in an organization, this method of measurement and assessment is also very popular in society at large. Bradburn and Sudman (1988) indicate that hundreds of thousands of surveys are conducted in the United States each year. The popularity of the survey method is further evidenced by the number of firms specializing in conducting surveys. Stanton (1989) estimates that nearly 2,000 U.S. survey research firms have total annual earnings of around $2 billion. This estimate does not include the extensive in-house use of surveys by private- and public-sector organizations. For example, the largest and most expensive survey in the world is the U.S. Census; it costs around $1 billion and is designed to obtain information on every person in the United States.

Although voting preference polls and surveys of general social attitudes receive most of the media attention, surveys have long been used in businesses, government agencies, universities, and other organizations (Rosenfeld et al., 1995). Organizational surveys began as a means of measuring employee morale in the years after World War II; subsequently, most organizations have conducted a company survey at least once (Hinrichs, 1991). In a poll of 429 human resource directors (Gallup, 1988), 70% of the respondents reported that their organizations had surveyed employees in the previous 10 years. Moreover, 69% of all respondents believed that they would conduct a survey in the future.

Organizational surveys appear to be increasing in popularity due to current management emphasis on employee involvement, customer satisfaction, total quality, and excellence in business practices (Barmash, 1993). As Rosenfeld, Doherty, Vicino, Kantor, and Greaves (1989) note,

> The current emphasis in managerial training on employee involvement in decision making has led to a resurgence in the use of surveys, as managers need to better understand the attitudes, beliefs, and opinions of employees before making decisions that affect their working lives. (p. 146)

Thus, the popularity of organizational surveys is due, to an extent, to the many and increasing uses these instruments have.

Uses of Surveys in Organizations

Organizational surveys can be constructed for many different purposes. This section examines three major uses of surveys: to gather information, to improve communication, and to evaluate the effectiveness of organizational change.[1]

Gathering Information

Well-conducted surveys allow an organization to gather accurate information on a wide range of issues. Often, no other data-gathering procedure can be used to collect the desired information (e.g., worker attitudes about a new retirement policy) more effectively or efficiently. As Wilmot and McClelland (1990) note, "suggestion systems, team meetings, and other forms of employee involvement do not necessarily provide workers with good opportunities to ask questions or raise concerns" (p. 72). For example, one popular type of organizational questionnaire, the exit survey, is often the only effective means of gathering data from a person whose employment with an organization is ending (Giacalone & Knouse, 1993). Exiting employees are surveyed because they often have important information about problems within the organization. Relative to their peers who are continuing to work in the organization, departing employees may be more willing to share such information. At the time of separation, departing employees no longer fear the repercussions of giving negative information on survey instruments. This low probability of reprisal results in less fear of reporting problems. Fear of reprisal is an issue that highlights an important distinction between organizational surveys versus those used for social, political polling, or marketing purposes. More specifically, organizational surveys may involve perceived risks to current employees who complete them. Despite the best guarantees of anonymity and confidentiality, some respondents may feel that they are potentially identifiable and could suffer negative consequences if their superiors become aware of any negative sentiments they choose to express.

A second and equally important information-gathering strength of organizational surveys is their flexibility. Organizational surveys can be used for many purposes, including assessing employees' needs, attitudes, morale, motivation, and work duties, as well as determining consumers' opinions and preferences about the goods and services they receive (Rosenfeld et al., 1995).[2]

Improving Communication

A survey can be a powerful tool to improve communication between different parts of an organization. Surveys are especially useful for establishing upward communication links from lower-level employees to management.

▥ *Establishing an Upward Communication Link*

Despite current corporate philosophies that emphasize open, two-way communication channels between management and employees, the burdens of supervisory roles often leave little time for open discussion or effective one-to-one communication (Wilmot & McClelland, 1990). Also, many employees may be reluctant to give management any bad news directly for fear of negative consequences. Johnson (1993) reports that only 29% to 41% of employees surveyed agreed that they say what is on their mind to management without fear of attack or reprisal. *U.S. News & World Report* (Dentzer, 1995) indicates that many low- and mid-level employees experience worker impotence. These employees feel that management ignores them, but the employees hesitate to speak up for fear of being fired. Two-thirds of those same people said they wanted to have more involvement in running their organizations.

Organizational surveys can provide employees with a direct and safe vehicle for communicating with upper management. Effective surveys give employees a feeling that they are a part of the decision-making process and that their input is important to the organization. This sense of empowerment may enhance employee motivation, organizational climate, and productivity (Rosenfeld et al., 1995).

The information gathered in a typical employee survey might include the needs and attitudes of organization members. For example, an anonymous survey could allow Ben (a low-level mailroom clerk), Elmer (an apprentice electrician), and Maria (an aspiring word processor) to communicate their training needs or how they feel about their supervisors to organizational decision makers without fear. Similarly, the ability to gather data from a wide spectrum of employees allows upper-level managers to keep their fingers on the pulse of the organization. Often, a survey is the only way to separate solid facts from rumor and innuendo and to ascertain systematically the prevalence of organizational problems. A survey allows management to assess, for example, whether the dissatisfactions with working conditions overheard in hushed tones in the hallways are the opinions and attitudes of a vocal disenchanted few or a much larger but quieter portion of the organization.

A second gain from this enhanced communication might be increased morale and motivation—an organizational quicker-picker-upper. When employees know that their opinions and needs are important to upper-level management, the stage is set for evolving into a more humane and productive organization—one where people really count. This benefit is risky, however, and can backfire because of organizational inertia. Policymakers risk compromising future survey efforts and alienating even the most loyal employees when they solicit information from employees and then do nothing with the results. The very act of conducting an organizational survey raises employees' expectations; doing nothing with survey results may lead to increased frustration, cynicism, and anger (Salemme, 1995). Thus, although organizational surveys can do many things, they cannot by themselves resolve problems or tell us whether management will act on the findings.

Monitoring and Evaluating the Effects of Organizational Change

Surveys administered at regular intervals (e.g., annually or biennially) offer an early detection system for upper-level management to spot changes in employee attitudes (Baron & Greenberg, 1990). The ability of upper-level management to deal with a negative change in attitudes at an early stage can minimize the turmoil that would have occurred had a situation been allowed to continue or worsen.

At other times, an organization may need to monitor the success of major interventions or the effect of new company programs and policies. For example, many companies are moving from an individual-based to a team-based approach to organizing work. Information obtained via surveys can facilitate the intervention process. Managers might want to use surveys to establish baselines (i.e., the levels of important characteristics before an intervention is begun). They may then want to gather survey data at three key steps in the change cycle: *unfreezing* (i.e., getting people to recognize the need for change), *changing* (i.e., attempting to create a new state of affairs), and *refreezing* (i.e., making the changes a permanent part of the organization's way of doing business; Lewin, 1947). By gathering survey data before an intervention begins and at each of these three steps, management can monitor and fine-tune the intervention to achieve optimum results. In this way, survey data can act as benchmarks to tell decision makers how they are progressing toward achieving organizational goals.

Factors to Consider Before Initiating the Survey Process

Although organizational surveys are used extensively, they are not the answer to every organizational problem. An organizational survey is a process, not a panacea. Surveys do not solve problems—they identify potential sources of problems and can act as catalysts for organizational change (Schiemann, 1991). As a result, surveys are a tool that should be used judiciously.

Four concerns are particularly important when determining whether a survey should be administered. First, the cost of doing a survey must be considered. Second, it should be kept in mind that specialized skills may be needed to conduct an effective and efficient survey. Third, other data-gathering methods should be examined to determine if they can deliver comparable data more quickly, less expensively, or with less organizational disruption. Fourth, overuse of surveys may have long-term negative effects.

Is a Survey Within the Organization's Budget?

Although the wealth of information an organizational survey provides may result in a long-term payoff, a well-done survey is not cheap. The actual total costs can be considerable. An organization incurs numerous direct labor and supply costs in the development, administration, analysis, and presentation phases of the survey process. In addition, there are indirect costs (e.g., respondent labor time) associated with conducting an organizational survey. These hidden costs may be greater than the direct costs. It is easy to overlook the indirect cost of the lost labor time incurred by each respondent who participates in a presurvey focus group or completes the survey on company time.[3] Maximizing survey benefits relative to costs occurs only when all the steps in the survey process are carefully followed.

Are Personnel With Survey Expertise Available?

A well-done survey usually requires personnel with skills in item writing, instrument development, sampling, and data analysis. If these personnel are not available within the organization, the use of external consultants for all or part of the survey process might be necessary. If the organization plans to conduct surveys on a regular basis, the most cost-effective approach might be to invest in survey-related training for designated personnel.

Are There Other Ways to Answer the Question?

The aphorism "If you give a child a hammer, everything suddenly will need hammering" also applies to surveys. There is a tendency to use the survey hammer on every organizational problem. Although we are strong advocates of surveys, they are not always the best way to assess organizational concerns. Depending on the particular situation, other data-gathering methods such as interviews, focus groups, quality circles, analyses of previously gathered data, observations, and work diaries or logs may be more appropriate.

The following example illustrates how various methods can be used to investigate a single organizational problem—absenteeism. If an organization is interested only in how much it spends per year in lost wages because of absenteeism, a computer program could easily count the number of absences per employee and multiply that by the person's daily wage and benefits. If, on the other hand, the organization is interested in the reasons for absenteeism, several methods and sources may be needed. These methods might include attitudinal data gathered via surveys, in-depth explanations for absenteeism obtained from individual interviews or focus groups, and a statistical analysis of the timing of absences (e.g., around weekends and holidays) extracted from organizational records.

Are Organizational Personnel Being Oversurveyed?

Organizational surveys may be suffering from the too-much-of-a-good-thing phenomenon. Kalton (1988) notes that "there has been considerable concern that the rate of total nonresponse has been increasing in recent years" (p. 116). Similarly, we (Edwards, Rosenfeld, Booth-Kewley, & Thomas, 1995) have found that potential respondents are less willing to complete and return surveys. We believe that part of this decline in the response rate—the percentage of surveys returned—can be attributed to the increased number of surveys being administered. Some people have told us that they are tired of receiving and completing surveys, especially when nothing is done about the problems they identify.

A related issue deals with increased skepticism of the survey process. Many individuals are bombarded with surveys at work, at home, and even when they go on vacation. Moreover, those who provide the data do not always see the payoffs. A survey may raise expectations that an organizational problem will be corrected. The disappointment and anger generated when negative situations remain may make employees less likely to respond to future surveys. For managers who are not committed to change, a survey may serve as a substitute for dealing with the actual problem. The survey effectively delays acting on difficult problems for several months or more. Our advice for those conducting an organizational survey is simple: Don't ask the questions unless you really want to know the answers and are prepared to follow through on the information you gather.

Setting the Table: Presurvey Issues

The Survey Team

Organizational surveys are complicated projects. Rarely will one person have the skills, knowledge, and time available to do it alone. We have found that the end product is better when a group of individuals known as a *survey team* works together in the design, administration, and analysis phases of the project.

▦ Choosing a Project Leader

A survey team should have a project leader. Having one person in charge of the survey team has several advantages. Assigning responsibility to a project leader enhances the likelihood that the project stays on course and on time because the leader can be held personally responsible if deadlines are not met. Authorizing one person to speak about the project ensures consistency when others in the organization have questions about the survey.

A team leader should minimally have expertise in either survey methods or the content area of the survey. The leader should also possess sufficient organizational clout to allow him or her to obtain all the needed resources (rooms, supplies, etc.) and have access to upper-level management (Schiemann, 1991). Even with expertise and clout, the leader must still rely heavily on others to gather the needed survey data.

▨ *Characteristics of the Survey Team*

Our recommendation for using a survey team acknowledges that multiple people are needed in most survey efforts. The different tasks involved in the various stages of the survey process require team members with complementary skills and characteristics. The characteristics needed to construct a good survey (e.g., item-writing skills and content-matter knowledge) are very different from the skills needed to administer the instrument (liaison and coordination function), process the data (data-entry skills), analyze the data (computer and statistical skills), or report the findings (writing or public speaking skills). Rarely will one individual possess a high level of skill in all these areas.

Using Internal Versus External Personnel to Conduct the Survey

A question that must be posed at the beginning of a survey is, "How much of the survey project will be done in-house?" A survey can be performed solely by in-house personnel, by a combination of internal and external personnel, or by external consultants or contractors with minimal in-house assistance. In a poll of 429 human resource directors (Gallup, 1988), 34% of the respondents reported that their firms did not use a consultant for any portion of their employee surveys. A common practice we have observed is to do the survey development and analysis in-house and to contract out functions such as mailing and data entry.

An example from our experience illustrates that poor use of internal personnel and resources can increase a survey's expense. For a survey being mailed to approximately 10,000 people, a supervisor had highly paid researchers stuff and subsequently open survey envelopes. Later, the same personnel keyed the data into the computer. A more cost-efficient procedure would have been to hire an external contractor to do the survey mailing and data-entry tasks. Using researchers to do these important but mundane tasks was overkill and, at around $25 an hour, an expensive proposition. In addition to being cheaper (by the hour), data-entry personnel who routinely enter data would have been faster (and probably more accurate) than the researchers.

Three factors affect the decision whether to use internal or external personnel: expertise, time, and expense. The first issue to determine is whether the organization has personnel with the necessary skills to conduct a survey. Second, if such personnel exist, can they be spared from other duties long enough to work on the survey project? The third issue is expense. Will it be more cost-effective to have in-house personnel conduct the survey or to use external consultants and contractors?

▨ *Conducting a Survey In-House*

If personnel with the appropriate skills are available to do the job, there are several reasons why an organization might choose to conduct the project entirely in-house. First, the data to be collected may be of a sensitive or proprietary nature. Although many external firms pride themselves on protecting their clients' privacy, a way to keep results from leaking to outsiders such as competitors or the media is to use in-house personnel. Second, internal personnel have a greater understanding of the organization. External firms may require large amounts of time from internal personnel to learn about the organization. Third, even if external personnel are brought in for the survey, internal personnel may play a major role in the survey project by coordinating meetings and data-gathering sessions.

■ *Hiring External Personnel to Conduct the Survey*

Consulting firms can be hired to do all or parts of an organizational survey. External consultants come from a wide variety of settings, ranging from firms that specialize in organizational surveys to university professors who moonlight as part-time consultants. Some organizations hire external consultants to perform all aspects of the survey process, while other organizations buy specific services (e.g., data entry and interviewing) or products (e.g., the survey itself or survey software).

Although the up-front costs charged by external consultants often seem excessive, external consultants can ultimately cost the organization less than the cost of doing the survey project totally in-house. External firms may complete the data gathering in less time and for less money than internal personnel, especially if the firm has extensive experience with surveys and already possesses specialized survey equipment or software. Consultants may lend credibility to the survey process, increasing the likelihood that management will take the results seriously and act on them (Schiemann, 1991). Because consultants are not full-time employees of the firm, some respondents may trust them more and feel less at risk than if the survey were administered by survey team members who are also employees.

Writing a Statement of Purpose

Before getting started, several important questions must be answered: Why is this survey being conducted? Who asked for it? What organizational problems, changes, or issues led up to this survey? What objectives are to be accomplished by the survey? What will the organization do with the survey results? We agree with Fowler's (1988) suggestion that survey designers start by writing a paragraph about what the instrument is supposed to accomplish. This statement of goals and purposes can be written by answering the questions we have just raised.

After the purpose statement is written, the team should be able to articulate clearly the objective(s) of the survey. If the team members cannot define each objective or different members view the survey as having different purposes, major problems may arise later. In the worst case, the team may discover that the collected data do not answer the question(s) that initiated the survey process.

Once the team has defined the objectives of the survey, it must make sure that management (or whoever is sponsoring the survey) shares the team's views. We have seen instances in which a survey team did an excellent job of designing and administering a survey that met the objectives but did little to meet the sponsor's needs.

The team should confer with the sponsor regarding the survey's objectives before taking further steps toward identifying content. Although some people may assume that most surveys are sponsored by an organization's top management, this does not appear to be the case. Only 39% of the human resources directors in a *Personnel Journal* poll reported that the survey was initiated by someone in senior management (Gallup, 1988). When human resources or middle- or lower-level employees are the ones suggesting the survey, a clear statement is needed to show upper management why the survey is necessary. If the purpose statement is not sufficiently convincing, upper-level management will probably not agree to the survey.

Conducting Organizational Surveys: A Look Ahead

The chapters that follow take the reader through the organizational survey process in a step-by-step fashion. After addressing the preliminary issues raised in this chapter, the next step is to define survey content. Chapter 2 describes the various methods for identifying and gathering survey content. These methods include interviews and focus groups, past surveys, published scales, and archival sources.

The core of any survey is its items. With the survey content defined in Chapter 2, procedures for writing items are discussed in Chapter 3. We review open- and closed-ended questions and describe three types of items: demographic, factual, and attitudinal. Although writing good items is more an art than a science, we provide rules that both novice and expert item writers are wise to follow.

Chapter 4 covers additional concerns that arise when writing items. To get good survey answers, it is important to choose or write good response alternatives. We describe a number of different response alternatives including multiple-choice, yes-no answers, and rating scales. Chapter 4 also deals with other nuts and bolts issues such as item order, survey length, and ways of controlling response bias.

For many people, the issue of how many respondents are needed for an organizational survey is a great mystery. Chapter 5 attempts to demystify the issue of selecting survey participants. We discuss whether a sample or everyone in the organization should be given the survey. In addition to describing various sampling strategies (e.g., simple random sampling and stratified sampling), we discuss sample size and sampling error.

Chapter 6 describes organizational survey administration. In organizations, surveys either can be given to individuals (to complete on their own) or can be administered in groups. There are also different modes of survey administration. Organizational surveys can be administered on paper, by computer, or through face-to-face and telephone interviews. Each of these administration modes has its proper uses, advantages, and disadvantages.

Regardless of the administration mode, common steps must be taken to get the survey into the field. Chapter 7 considers issues such as the survey introduction, cover letter, and instructions, as well as pretesting the survey and obtaining organizational approval for the final instrument. In addition to these general issues, there are other concerns when surveys are distributed through the mail. These issues include preparing, assembling, and distributing the survey packet and whether to send the survey through office mail or through a postal service.

After the survey has been distributed, the issue of respondents' willingness to complete and return the survey arises. Chapter 8 describes how to calculate a response rate and what an acceptable response rate is. Nonresponse bias is defined and explained. Because low response rates can impair the quality of survey data, ways to maximize response rates are described. These methods include prenotification, follow-ups, incentives, and making the survey meaningful.

When surveys have been returned, the data need to be coded and entered. Chapter 9 describes the nitty-gritty of data coding, entry, and cleaning. It also reviews methods for dealing with missing data. Finally, ways of categorizing and coding responses to open-ended survey items are described.

Once the data have been coded and entered, analysis begins. Chapter 10 considers the various ways organizational survey data are analyzed and interpreted. Frequencies, percentages, means and standard deviations, and methods of analyzing differences between subgroups are discussed.

Chapter 11 describes presentation of survey findings to management, employees, and anyone else who will listen. Techniques for presenting the survey's background, method, results, conclusions, and recommendations are discussed. We conclude with some practical advice for ensuring that the results of the survey are clearly understood and the findings become the basis for organizational change.[4]

Notes

1. Organizational surveys can also be used to test hypotheses (e.g., Do women prefer team-oriented work environments more than men do?), to evaluate programs (e.g., How effective is a new worker safety training program?), and as part of needs assessment studies (e.g., How much foreign language schooling do employees transferring to an overseas work site need?).

2. Although customer surveys are beyond the scope of this book, it is important to note that many organizations increasingly use surveys to establish communication with external customers. Everywhere consumers turn today, they are faced with surveys asking them to evaluate the goods and services they receive. One reason for this renewed emphasis on customer satisfaction surveys is the total quality management (TQM) movement that has taken hold in many industries. A key aspect of TQM is the need for constant improvement through satisfying the customer's needs. Surveys are used by TQM proponents to solicit information from employees (the individuals who are most intimately familiar with the making of a product or the delivery of a service) and customers (the individuals who use the goods and services). With the publication of the National Performance Review, customer satisfaction surveys also became a major

undertaking in the U.S. federal government. On September 11, 1993, President Clinton issued Executive Order 12862, *Setting Customer Service Standards* (White House, 1993). This executive order establishes three survey tasks that government agencies are required to conduct periodically: surveys of customers to determine the kind and quality of services wanted, surveys of customers to assess satisfaction with current services, and surveys of frontline employees to identify barriers preventing the government from matching the quality levels achieved by business (Coffey, 1993).

3. The total costs for even a relatively small-scale survey can be surprisingly high. For a hypothetical 120-item survey given to 500 employees, Scarpello and Vandenberg (1991) estimate direct costs of $15,000 (500 employees multiplied by $30 per employee to administer, process, and analyze the surveys) and indirect costs of $16,560 (average hourly salary plus benefits of $16.56 per hour multiplied by 2 hours for administration, feedback, and going to and from the administration site, multiplied by 500 employees). The total survey cost of $31,560 translates into a per employee survey cost of $63.12!

4. As we were completing this book, Kraut's (1996) edited volume on organizational surveys was published. It contains chapters providing in-depth discussions of many of the topics covered in this book including steps in the survey process, administration methods, data collection and analysis, survey feedback, and linking results to change.

Identifying
Survey Content

2

If the survey team is to develop a short questionnaire that addresses only one or two dimensions (e.g., satisfaction with the company's compensation system, whether the current retirement system should be changed), determining the survey content should be a relatively straightforward task. On the other hand, a survey of organizational climate (a topic with many dimensions) or an instrument to diagnose a complex organizational problem (e.g., high employee turnover or absenteeism) requires more effort to identify survey content.

Methods for Identifying Survey Content

Many different sources and techniques are available for identifying the content of a survey. Before starting to write the survey, the team should consider all the possible methods for identifying content and should use the methods that best fit the purpose(s) of the survey and the needs of the organization. The most popular methods for identifying survey content include developmental interviews, focus groups, past surveys in the same organization, published scales, archival sources, academic literature, and other sources such as governmental agencies and professional colleagues.

Although we describe each way of identifying survey content individually, using a number of methods rather than just one is usually preferred. We often supplement organization-specific information with content from both scientifically based reviews of the literature and previously published scales. For example, to identify information for a survey of workplace safety, each team member might be assigned one or more of the following activities: examining personnel records such as accident reports, conducting focus group interviews with supervisors and job incumbents who have or have not been injured recently on the job, and reviewing the scientific literature. Insights provided by each technique may make the survey team consider topics and perspectives that otherwise might not have been investigated.

A word of caution: It is generally a good idea to limit the scope of an organizational survey. A common beginner's error is to include too many topics on a single survey (Scarpello & Vandenberg, 1991). Trying to cover many topics on a survey can prove as problematic as having too few.

Developmental Interviews and Focus Groups

Developmental interviews and focus groups (which are basically group interviews) are popular means of gathering information for survey developers. Interviews and focus groups allow team members to solicit information from people who have a variety of perspectives related to the purpose of the survey. They help identify the jargon peculiar to a particular workplace so that the survey can be written in a language that is meaningful to respondents. These techniques can also serve as public relations tools. Giving organizational players an opportunity to add their input may convince them and their peers of the survey's relevance and the need to complete the questionnaire when it is administered.

Developmental interviews and focus groups can also help determine what issues should not be included in the survey because not much can be done to change them. As Verheyen (1988) notes, "soliciting information in an area about which management is intractable is only an exercise in frustration for all concerned" (p. 74). Sahl (1990) states that considerable harm can be done by falsely raising organization members' hopes that something will be done about problems that top management will not or cannot address because of company policies or a lack of resources. Determining these off-limits issues at this initial stage of instrument development will avoid wasted efforts.

Interviews need to be used appropriately because they are labor intensive. Both interviews and focus groups take personnel away from performing their real job functions. When being interviewed, salespeople cannot contact customers, production employees cannot produce, and managers cannot supervise their subordinates and projects. Also, scheduling and conducting interviews and focus groups is time consuming. If an interviewer needs to go to multiple sites in several cities or countries, the survey construction process will be slowed considerably.

The wealth of information that comes from interviews and focus groups should more than compensate for the costs and time they require. The payoffs can be higher productivity, greater commitment, increased morale, or other organizational benefits that result from the survey.

▦ *Developmental Interviews*

An important early step in identifying the content for any survey is conducting individual developmental interviews with those in the know— top management or key personnel (Schiemann, 1991). By getting to top management early, the survey team can minimize potential miscommunications that might result in developing an instrument that is unacceptable. Also, interviewing members of top management is a way to increase their commitment to the survey. Without this commitment, the best survey in the world may ultimately be doomed and its results ignored. Wilmot and McClelland (1990) advise the survey team to "scrap the project" at this stage if top executives are not committed to taking actions based on survey results.

Before beginning, the team should inform participants of the interview purpose. To make the purpose more concrete, a team member might want to provide future interviewees with some sample questions to consider. Providing this foundation for the interview gives participants an opportunity to organize their thoughts and ask peers for their inputs. Also, the interviewees should be told how long the session will last. Typically, the interviews last from 30 to 90 minutes, depending on the level of the personnel being interviewed, the number of interviewees, and the purpose of the survey. No more than two interviewees should be present at each session, especially in developmental interview with top management.

The interviewer should have a number of prepared questions. The initial question list may evolve from survey team discussion or a review of related surveys and studies. Information gathered from early interviews should then be used to develop additional questions for subsequent sessions. The ordering of the questions should be from the most general to the most specific, a procedure known as *funneling* (O'Brien, 1993). The interviewer should generally avoid questions that can be answered with a simple yes or no. Probes such as "Tell me more about . . ." or "Why do you think . . ." are good ways to solicit in-depth information and to draw reluctant participants into the conversation (Stewart & Shamdasani, 1990). Finally, the interviewer should periodically provide feedback on the points that have been made to ensure that the information being recorded reflects interviewees' concerns and perspectives accurately.

▓ *Focus Groups* Because time and money can be saved by conducting interviews in groups rather than with individuals, focus groups have become an extremely popular technique for identifying survey content. Focus groups are extensively used by marketing researchers testing consumer preferences, or researchers investigating what determines a successful advertising campaign, and political consultants seeking evidence of a candidate's popularity (Frey & Fontana, 1993; Kolbert, 1992). Still, as Morgan (1993) notes, "the best known use of focus groups in combination with other methods has been as a preliminary step in the development of survey instruments" (p. xii).

Two types of focus groups are applicable to organizational surveys. The most common and important is the *presurvey focus group.* This technique allows the team to get acquainted with survey topics that they themselves may not know much about and to develop the specific content areas, items, and response categories that will be on the actual survey (O'Brien, 1993). Focus groups can also be used to test preliminary survey items. Participants can be asked to evaluate the appropriateness of the questions, the clarity of question wording, and the comprehensiveness of the response options. After the survey data have been analyzed, the team may decide to conduct *postsurvey focus groups*. This technique provides further explanations about what the survey results mean and how changes based on the results can be implemented (Stewart & Shamdasani, 1990).

It usually takes two members of the survey team to conduct a focus group. A leader asks the questions and controls the flow and direction of the discussion, and a recorder takes detailed notes about the responses (Scarpello & Vandenberg, 1991). In a simple organizational model, the leader begins the session by indicating that the purpose of the focus group is to obtain information that will help the team develop items for a survey. The leader then suggests some topics (e.g., career development, job satisfaction, working environment) that top management identified in the developmental interviews. Each member of the group is then asked in turn to indicate how he or she feels about these topics. Next, the leader asks a number of general or specific questions about the various topic areas. After all participants have supplied their input, the recorder reads back a summary of the comments. This last step provides participants with a chance to correct any errors that the recorder made and to add to or refine previous statements (Scarpello & Vandenberg, 1991).

With sensitive topics, anonymity and confidentiality may be difficult if not impossible to guarantee because other members of the group may act as moles. This is important for the leader to realize because some focus group participants may be reluctant to share their true views if they believe this information could come back to haunt them (Wilmot & McClelland, 1990).

Another concern, noted by Wilmot and McClelland (1990), is that some focus group participants might be reluctant to talk because their peers may "disapprove of them if they express their concerns honestly" (p. 71). These problems can be reduced by not placing members of the same work group or department in the same focus group, by not using last names, and by promising that taped transcripts will not be distributed.

Alternative focus group procedures may lessen these problems. These procedures might include having respondents write answers to sensitive items on cards, collecting and shuffling the cards, reading each anonymous comment, and then asking for discussion of each comment. Box 2.1 provides another variation of the focus group method that is designed to enhance anonymity.

It is important that the leader conduct the focus group in a nonjudgmental way (Stewart & Shamdasani, 1990), appearing neither to agree nor to disagree with responses. This may require some willpower if the statements are extreme or prejudicial. For example, one of our colleagues conducted focus groups to identify the survey content for a study on the integration of women into traditionally male, blue-collar jobs. She assured all focus group members that they could speak freely about any problems

BOX 2.1

Generating Survey Content for Sensitive Issues

While some people become liberated by the group dynamics of the focus group and freely give their views, others may be inhibited by group pressure to conform or by the status of other members. These inhibitory forces can be especially strong when sensitive topics are discussed (e.g., quality of supervision, substance abuse, views on affirmative action). In these cases, the survey team may want to modify the focus-group methodology and use an alternative, less-evaluative technique to generate survey content and items.

One such method is the nominal group technique (NGT). As a survey-development technique, NGT involves each group member first being interviewed individually about the survey topics. Responses are then summarized by the interviewer. These summaries are distributed to all members of the focus group at a later meeting (Stewart & Shamdasani, 1990). At that meeting, the key issues are listed by the leader on a blackboard or butcher paper. The leader has the group discuss which items need to be rephrased, eliminated because of redundancy, and so on. The group generates a final list of issues that they believe should be investigated with regard to the original

purpose of the survey. In some instances, the focus-group members may also be asked to rank-order or in some other way indicate the most important issues. In this way, the original ideas can be discussed, expanded, discarded, and revised without anyone knowing who proposed them in the first place.

Giacalone and Knouse (1993) described a modified version of the NGT for developing an exit survey dealing with security issues. Because of the sensitive nature of the topic, they first had their participants privately write about known or potential monitary crimes that they had seen or heard of in their company. The participants also wrote descriptions of organizational practices that they thought made the company vulnerable to security problems. The group members individually presented their written ideas, which were then summarized and categorized on flip charts by the leader. To avoid inhibiting the discussion, the focus was on idea-clarification rather than idea-evaluation. At the end, the group members voted on the items that they thought were the most likely security issues or problems. These results were used to develop the exit survey.

they saw with women working in organizational positions similar to theirs. After a number of rather innocuous comments, one participant in an all-male focus group said words to the effect of "You know how women are during 'that time of the month.' You just can't manage them!" The leader said nothing even though that opinion was very different from her own.

We strongly advocate using presurvey focus groups during the initial period of content identification. Although there are various opinions on the composition of a focus group, the general consensus is that each focus group should consist of between 6 and 12 people who are members of the population that will later be surveyed (Fowler, 1993; Schiemann, 1991). Smaller groups may not capture the full range of inputs from organizational members; groups larger than 12 may be difficult to control (Stewart & Shamdasani, 1990). The number of focus groups that should be run depends on the size and structure of the organization as well as the number and nature of the topics being surveyed. A good working rule is to capture the views of most major subgroups or entities within the organization. When focus group responses become repetitive, it probably means that enough focus groups have been conducted.

In building focus groups, the survey team needs to choose participants carefully. Sometimes, focus group members are selected for reasons of convenience. For example, survey team members might be tempted to choose friends, acquaintances, or people in nearby work spaces. Instead, focus groups should include representatives of all subgroups of interest to the organization. Sahl (1990) suggests having upper management identify relevant subgroups during developmental interviews. Management should not, however, be allowed to select individual focus group participants.

Subgroups identified for the focus groups will be useful later when the survey team defines its target population and begins planning data analyses. These subgroups are identified by factors such as organizational level (e.g., middle management vs. hourly worker), gender, race, age, functional area of the organization (such as production or marketing), and unit location (e.g., headquarters vs. branch facility). Given that each focus group participant will vary on multiple factors (e.g., an African American woman who works in a branch production facility), a relatively small number of organizational members can cover a wide variety of target subgroups. The point is that the perspectives of all the potential survey respondents should be reflected in the composition of the focus groups and subsequently in the survey content.

O'Brien (1993) suggests that each focus group should be homogeneous in terms of race, gender, or other important demographic characteristics to encourage more candid responses. In our experience, using homogeneous groups is essential only if responses to potential survey topics might be expected to vary greatly for one or more of the demographic groups. For example, if the team is developing a survey assessing sexual harassment, it makes sense to run separate male and female focus groups. There is less need to do so for a survey of organizational climate or job satisfaction. We do agree with Schiemann (1991), however, that supervisors and subordinates should not be in the same focus group. Differences in power may restrict those lower in status from freely expressing their views.

Finally, focus groups should generally not be used with top management or other key organizational players. As senior leaders, they may be uncomfortable talking candidly about sensitive organizational issues as part of a group. Developmental interviews are most appropriately conducted with these individuals.

▥ *Using Interview Information*

Once the developmental and focus group interviews have been conducted, the team needs to turn the raw material into survey categories, items, and response alternatives. Stewart and Shamdasani (1990) recommend the *cut-and-paste method.* With this method, the survey team reviews interview notes and identifies categories that correspond to the key topics, phrases, words, and issues raised by the participants. Each section of the notes that corresponds to each category is marked with a different color. At the end of the process, the categories that are similar are cut and pasted together. Using the item-writing guidelines described in Chapters 3 and 4, focus group participants' own words and phrases can be used to generate items and response alternatives within the chosen categories (O'Brien, 1993).

Past Surveys in the Same Organization

Past surveys conducted by the same organization are excellent sources of content when developing a new survey. Findings from past surveys may also serve as a baseline for interpreting the results of the current survey. Even if the organization has never conducted a survey measuring all the exact same content areas, the team should look at the dimensions and items used in prior surveys. Seeing the items, dimensions, and results from past surveys may give the team valuable clues on what the current survey should include.

A survey team should not, however, use items and scales from past surveys just because it is convenient to do so. If the current survey's purpose is very different from that of a prior survey, the new instrument will most likely require different questions and scales. Even if the stated purpose is the same, it should not be assumed that the prior survey actually accomplished its objectives. Readministering an old survey in its entirety may appear time- and cost-effective, but the organization may find that the survey did not fully address the concerns that necessitated it in the first place. In one case, employees leaving a large organization completed an exit survey that had been developed 10 years before. In the intervening period, the organization had made many changes and taken steps to correct several of the reasons (e.g., low pay, poor benefits, lack of job security) for voluntary resignation. When the survey was readministered, the organization learned little. The decade-old survey no longer captured the most important current reasons for departure.[1]

Published Scales

For many reasons, a survey team might want to use or adapt items from scales or surveys found in published studies (Bourque & Clark, 1992). One, the team might want to see how its population is similar or different from other groups. Two, the experitise to construct a better measure might not exist in the organization. Three, the reliability and validity of the previously published scales are already known. For a home-grown survey or scale, these indicators will not be known until after the survey is over, when it may be too late.[2] Finally, the organization may need data immediately. Using a previously developed scale could save valuable time.

Even if the team decides that it does not want to adopt a scale as is, it might want to adapt a published scale to fit its needs. For example, a published instrument might be adapted to make it more relevant to the current organization. Items developed on college students or other samples might need to be amended to reflect the culture, policies, and terminology of the organization that will be surveyed. Including all the items from a previously developed survey instrument is often not desirable because the prior instrument may not have been designed to accomplish the goals of the current survey. The team must carefully determine the content areas that the current survey should address, rather than simply use the ones that happen to appear on an existing instrument.

▦ *Scales Contained in Compendia* The professional literature contains a wealth of information on organizational survey topics such as job satisfaction, pay and benefits, work motivation, and organizational climate. One easy way to access this information is to consult compendia that contain numerous instruments organized by content areas. In addition to listing the items, these compendia often provide evaluative information (e.g., reliability) on the scales.

Bourque and Clark (1992) list some volumes (Chun, Cobb, & French, 1975; McDowell & Newell, 1987; Reeder, Ramacher, & Gorelnik, 1976; Robinson, Shaver, & Wrightsman, 1991; Shaw & Wright, 1967) that contain scales that might be of use in organizational surveys. Other volumes (e.g., British Telecom, 1984a, 1984b; Miller, 1991; Robinson, Athanasiou, & Head, 1969) are also available. The team may profit from a quick review of the library holdings of a major university or by searching the information superhighway using the Internet or the World Wide Web. For instance, many researchers and survey practitioners obtain valuable free help by placing questions such as "Can anyone suggest a scale to measure . . . ?" on e-mail discussion groups (e.g., the Academy of Management's HRNET, administered through Cornell University) devoted to organizational issues.

Because compendia typically emphasize the collection of scales in established and well-researched areas, survey teams investigating new areas (e.g., workers' attitudes toward corporate reengineering) would also benefit from an examination of recent empirical research. Most college and university libraries have CD-ROM databases (e.g., PSYCHLIT, ABI INFORM) that can be searched for abstracts of research studies in the organizational behavior and psychological sciences.

Frequently, the items in compendia and periodicals are in the public domain. That is, people who wish to use the items are free to do so. It is a good idea, however, to contact the journal or book publishers and the authors when there is any question about whether survey items are copyrighted.

In rare cases, the authors of survey scales ask for a copy of the data in exchange for free use of their instrument. The team needs to decide whether surrendering data is too high a price for the use of the published scales. The survey team should check with top management before promising to release data. Releasing data on the entire survey or even a single dimension may be against organizational policies.

▩ *Commercially Available Surveys*

The wide variety of commercially available surveys provides organizations with other instruments to meet many generic assessment and diagnostic needs. Depending on the survey, these commercially available instruments may have any or all of the following advantages: immediate availability for administration, norms against which the company's results can be compared, and rigorous development.

Because commercially available surveys are developed for a wide range of organizations, such instruments may not assess some of the dimensions of interest to the organization, or they may address the issues too globally. Sahl (1990) is particularly critical of the use of standardized questionnaire items. He suggests that using overly general questions on an organizational survey might cause the survey to lose credibility in the eyes of respondents.

When using commercially available instruments, the team may have to pay for permission to use survey items. When such an expense is involved, the team must decide whether the costs are worth the benefit of being able to use the desired items. If the scales are to be part of a recurring survey (e.g., an annual assessment of job satisfaction) or require a per respondent fee for a large-scale survey, the organization will probably be better served by developing its own scale.

Archival Sources

The administration of a survey is often prompted by an organizational problem such as employee turnover, absenteeism, or the need to redesign jobs. In such cases, the survey team could obtain valuable information about the problem from materials readily available in the organization. Examples of such documentation include company policies and handbooks, annual reports, job descriptions, personnel records, injury reports, training manuals, and performance evaluations. Table 2.1 shows how some of these sources might be used to identify the content of surveys.

Table 2.1 highlights two important points:

1. Many types of archival data are relevant in identifying the content of a survey.
2. People who think about surveys only in terms of employee attitude measurement severely limit the usefulness of this organizational assessment tool.

Theory and Academic Findings

Many organizational personnel and survey practitioners get queasy at the mention of theory, models, and empirical studies and, consequently, often avoid using theory when developing applied organizational surveys. An automatic rejection of these tools as being too academic may limit the quality of the survey. Using theory and academic findings as guides in identifying the survey content can enhance the quality of the survey and may help the organization see how the issues the survey addresses fit together into a bigger picture.

Organization X is having a problem with absenteeism in its production department; how can academic research play a role in identifying survey

TABLE 2.1 Using Archival Data to Identify Survey Content

Organizational Need Addressed in a Survey	*Potentially Relevant Archival Data*
Task Inventory	▩ Existing job descriptions ▩ Training manuals ▩ Narratives from performance evaluations
Safety Enhancement	▩ Injury reports ▩ Narratives from performance evaluations
Absenteeism	▩ Personnel records (e.g., excused absences) ▩ Company policies on absenteeism

content? Management assumes that the high rate of absenteeism is due to job dissatisfaction and therefore directs a survey team to develop and administer a measure of job satisfaction. The team examines the academic literature on work absenteeism and discovers that there is not a consistent relationship between job satisfaction and absenteeism (Saal & Knight, 1988). Furthermore, the team learns that a number of important factors (ranging from work-family conflict to organizational policies on absenteeism to demographic variables) are correlated with absenteeism. The team concludes that the survey scope should be expanded to include these factors. If the academic literature on absenteeism had not been consulted, it is unlikely that this broadening of the survey content would have occurred.

Reviewing past and current theory on the topics covered in the survey can help the team make better decisions about the survey content. Theory can serve as a guide to areas and items on which the survey should focus. The survey team may also find it useful to learn how others measured the content areas that its survey will be assessing. Although examination of the theoretical and academic literature can be time consuming, we have found that the payoff in improved survey quality usually makes it time well spent.

Other Sources of Survey Content

In addition to these traditional ways of identifying survey content, there are other sources that can be used. By networking with peers in different organizations, the survey team may learn how these organizations addressed comparable problems and may be able to obtain copies of surveys used for similar purposes. Verheyen (1988) correctly notes that concerns addressed in other organizations' surveys are frequently the same as those found in the survey team's organization.

An organization may want to consider joining or starting a consortium that conducts organizational surveys. A consortium is a group whose members represent the interests of their own respective organizations and agree to cooperate according to some agreed-on rules to help all the member companies become more competitive (Morris & LoVerde, 1993). In the case of a survey consortium, the member organizations may administer a complete instrument or, more commonly, a set of core questions shared by all consortium members and incorporated into their own unique surveys. Member companies also share data they obtain from the common set of survey questions. The advantages of this process include decreased survey development costs and standards (i.e., survey norms) against which the performance of the member organizations can be compared.

In addition to a survey consortium, regional and national associations (e.g., the local chamber of commerce) are other external sources that can assist a survey team. These organizations often have a great deal of archival data available. In addition to being useful for identifying survey content areas, such data often can place an organization's survey findings in context (e.g., comparing the results for a particular organization with regional or national findings on the same issue). In some cases, these associations may be willing to act as external survey consultants (Scarpello & Vandenberg, 1991).

Government agencies are another source of inexpensive external assistance. For example, Sheatsley (1983) advocates using the definitions, questions, and answer categories used by the U.S. Census Bureau whenever possible. Also, reports issued by federal research laboratories (e.g., Army Research Institute), the General Accounting Office, other government agencies (e.g., U.S. Merit Systems Protection Board), and major government contractors (e.g., the RAND Corporation) address a wide range of organizational issues. Reports from these organizations often include findings, a copy of the actual survey or other data-gathering instruments, and a description of the methods used to gather the data. Adapting portions of the instruments and procedures could save considerable time and money.

Conclusions

In sum, the survey team has a wide variety of methods and sources that can be used to identify survey content. In most situations, no one method or source provides all the needed information. Before starting to write the survey, the team should consider all the possible methods for identifying survey content and use those that best fit the needs of the organization and the desired time frame of the survey.

Notes

1. Written comments from the organization's prior surveys can offer another excellent source for developing new items and new dimensions. If multiple respondents wrote about similar issues, the survey team should consider addressing these issues in a future survey (if not with postsurvey focus groups). Statistical findings from a prior administration of a recurring survey also can determine whether some content areas should be deemphasized, remain unchanged, or be studied in more depth. Similarly, the statistical

analysis of one administration of a survey can tell the survey team if additional or fewer items are needed to get a reliable assessment of a content area.

2. Although many published scales may have more rigorous development than scales from home-grown instruments, this developmental rigor does not always translate into more validity. In their meta-analytic review of organizational development studies, Neuman, Edwards, and Raju (1989) found that organization-specific attitude instruments actually had a significantly higher average validity coefficient than did validity coefficients from published instruments. This finding suggests that researchers and survey developers should show a healthy dose of skepticism before adopting a well-developed generic scale. A home-grown scale that hones in on the issues at hand may be much better at measuring and predicting the behaviors of concern in that particular organization.

Creating the Survey, Part I
Writing Survey Items

3

No other aspect of the survey process is probably more important than writing survey items. Items are the building blocks of the survey. The way the survey questions perform—the adequacy with which they obtain the desired information—has a greater influence on the results of the survey than any other single part of the process. Accordingly, great care should go into the writing of survey items. This chapter focuses on writing individual survey items. In the next chapter, we discuss various response formats and scales that respondents use to answer survey questions. The order of these two chapters is arbitrary because the survey team must know the information in both these chapters before translating the information discussed in Chapter 2 into complete survey items.

Item Formats: Closed- and Open-Ended Questions

Survey questions fall into two general categories: closed ended and open ended. *Closed-ended questions* ask respondents to choose from a fixed set of response alternatives. Examples of closed-ended questions include multiple-choice, yes-no, and questions with a numerical rating scale. *Open-ended questions,* on the other hand, ask for an answer in the respondent's own words. Fill-ins, short-answers, and essays are examples of this type of item.

Closed-Ended Questions

Closed-ended (or structured) items provide response alternatives from which survey respondents must choose. The response alternatives may be in the form of a numerical rating scale such as 1 = Strongly disagree to 5 = Strongly agree, a simple yes-no format, or a set of categories in a multiple-choice format. For instance, to answer the question, "During the past 3 months, which of the following types of performance feedback did you receive from your supervisors?", a respondent might be asked to select one of the following multiple-choice alternatives: (a) Oral and written feedback, (b) Oral feedback only, (c) Written feedback only, or (d) No feedback.

▦ *Advantages* The many advantages of closed-ended items make this format very popular in organizational surveys. Respondents usually find closed-ended questions fast and easy to answer, a very important consideration in the time-is-money organizational world. It takes considerably less effort to check a box, select an alternative, or rate something on a 1-to-5 scale than to think of and write a narrative answer. In addition, closed-ended questions are easy to code and process, especially when computer administration or scannable answer forms are used.

Another important advantage of closed-ended questions is that they restrict the range of possible responses to those pertinent to the goals of the survey. Closed-ended questions communicate the same frame of reference to everyone, allowing respondents to perform the task of interpreting the question and potential answers more reliably. Because of this common frame of reference, individuals who complete the survey are likely to read and interpret closed-ended items in the same way.

Closed-ended questions typically provide respondents with cues for retrieving information from memory. The list of response options presented with closed-ended items often reminds respondents of information they might otherwise have forgotten (Bradburn & Sudman, 1991). For example, consider the following question: "During the past 12 months, which company-sponsored training programs did you attend?" A closed-ended question provides a list of all training programs sponsored. Without a list of such memory cues, respondents might supply only a partial record of the training programs they attended.

▦ *Disadvantages* Closed-ended items also have drawbacks. A common criticism is that closed-ended questions force people to choose among response alternatives that may not reflect their real feelings about the topic. Responses to closed-ended items may be unduly influenced by the specific alternatives provided. In addition, forcing people to choose a fixed answer that best matches their actual response cannot always capture subtle but sometimes important distinctions among respondents.

Closed-ended questions may compel people to express an attitude when they have no opinion on the matter or, even worse, when they do not understand the question. Also, if all or nearly all the questions on the survey are closed ended, some respondents may be frustrated by not being allowed to express their views in their own words. One of our job satisfaction surveys consisted of only closed-ended questions. Some people told us later that they felt the items did not fully capture all aspects of the topics about which they were asked. The respondents felt that they were forced to answer in set ways and were not allowed to express their true points of view.

How can the survey team avoid such criticism? Judicious use of open-ended questions may provide the answer.

Open-Ended Questions

Open-ended items (also called *unstructured items*) require respondents to supply survey answers in their own words (Alreck & Settle, 1985). Responses to open-ended questions are often given in narrative form (such as an essay), although some open-ended questions such as "How many people are there in your work group?" require short answers in the form of numerical data.

■ *Advantages*

The narrative information obtained from open-ended questions can add flesh to the sometimes sterile numbers and deductions drawn from responses to closed-ended items. Responses to open-ended questions often convey information that cannot be derived from responses to a fixed set of prespecified answers. They also may be a better means of obtaining information about sensitive, controversial, or taboo topics (Converse & Presser, 1986) such as substance abuse or employee sabotage. This information may provide insights into the issues important to employees and management, give suggestions for organizational changes, and provide material for future surveys.

One of the biggest advantages of open-ended questions is that they allow respondents to answer using their own frame of reference, without undue influence from prespecified alternatives (Sheatsley, 1983). Because of this, open-ended questions may elicit responses that describe more closely the real views of those completing the survey. The respondents' answers to open-ended questions reflect both the content and the salience or priority of their concerns. Narrative answers additionally provide a more in-depth assessment of respondents' attitudes on a topic than is usually possible with closed-ended questions.

An important and often overlooked advantage of open-ended items is that they allow respondents to blow off steam or ventilate their feelings on emotion-laden topics (e.g., downsizing, performance appraisal system). Even when open-ended responses do not prove useful in identifying problems, respondents often appreciate the opportunity to express their feelings. The open-ended format may elicit information that would never have surfaced had respondents been forced to choose from a list of answers. In addition, allowing people to write narrative answers acknowledges that they may possess information that is important and relevant, but that was not covered in the closed-ended survey items.

Another advantage of open-ended items is that they provide responses in a form that many managers appreciate. Managers often like to hear responses given in employees' own words and feel that these narrative answers provide key insights into the beliefs and attitudes of their organizational members. Such comments may be the only way that issues are presented to upper-level managers in the language used by personnel.

■ *Disadvantages*

Open-ended survey items come with a price. A survey filled with open-ended questions may take a lot of time to complete, especially if long narratives are required. As a result, questions placed toward the end of the survey may receive perfunctory treatment due to fatigue. In addition, a certain percentage of respondents may refuse to fill out some or all of the open-ended items due to the effort involved.

From the survey team's point of view, the biggest disadvantage is the time and effort required to process and analyze answers to open-ended questions. Although open-ended questions are easier to compose than closed-ended questions because the survey team does not have to write response alternatives or construct a response scale, the effort saved may be minimal compared to what is required to read or code the narrative responses to open-ended items. If a survey with several open-ended questions is administered to a large group of respondents, the delay between survey administration and the presentation of the results could be substantial.

An additional drawback of open-ended questions is that they are not an effective way to measure intensity of opinion or satisfaction about a topic. If assessment of intensity is a goal of the survey, questions that use a rating scale or multiple-choice options would be preferable to open-ended items.

Another problem associated with open-ended questions is that individuals vary widely in their ability to write narrative answers. Differences in responses may reflect differences in ability to express opinions as much as real differences in shades of opinion (Sheatsley, 1983). We have found that junior or blue-collar employees typically do not write as many or as extensive comments as do managerial, white-collar, and better-educated employees who sometimes write several pages. One of our colleagues learned this lesson when she administered an organizational climate survey at a facility where most of the respondents were highly educated engineers. She was surprised that a number of the engineers showed up at the administration site carrying typed notes expressing their comments about the topics to be surveyed before they had been given the actual survey! At the other extreme, open-ended questions almost inevitably elicit a certain amount of illegible, irrelevant, incoherent, and repetitious information from respondents.

A better method for obtaining qualitative information in a controlled fashion is to ask respondents to list the three best and worst things associated with an issue, or the three most important reasons they think a certain organizational problem has occurred. For example, if an organization is administering a survey to understand its employee turnover problem, the survey might ask respondents to list the three most important reasons why employees are leaving the organization.

Should the Survey Team Use Closed- or Open-Ended Questions?

Given that both of these general item formats have advantages and disadvantages, what type should be used on an organizational survey? One solution is to allow room for one or more open-ended explanations to supplement the information gained from the closed-ended question. The following example illustrates that strategy:

Did you use the organization's on-site health facility during the past 6 months?

___ Yes___ No

If your answer was No, please explain why you chose not to use the facility.

_____

_____

Even though many survey books conclude that closed-ended items are preferable to open-ended items, it is usually a good idea to include one or more open-ended items at the end of the survey. The open-ended items allow respondents the opportunity to add relevant information in their own words. Even if no open-ended questions are included in the body of the survey, we recommend that an item asking for general comments ("Do you have any other comments about the topics covered in this survey? If yes, please indicate them in the space below.") be placed at the end of the survey.

We usually limit open-ended questions to situations in which we do not know enough about the possible issues to write appropriate response alternatives, and situations in which the list of possible answers or categories is longer than is feasible to present to respondents. We also sometimes allow room for general comments after main sections of the survey or at the very end of the questionnaire.

Item Content: Demographic, Factual, and Attitudinal Questions

Items vary in content as well as form. Survey items may be thought of as falling into three general content categories: demographic, factual, and attitudinal. Each of these item types can be open or closed ended. *Demographic items* ask respondents for information about their backgrounds (e.g., gender, job title, work department). *Factual items* ask about respondents' behaviors or experiences (e.g., "How many sick days did you take during the past year?") and other facts within respondents' realm of experience (e.g., "Did you attend safety training during the past year?"). *Attitudinal items* ask for respondents' attitudes, opinions, beliefs, or perceptions on a topic ("To what extent do you agree or disagree that this organization's performance evaluation system is fair?").

Demographic Items

Demographic items provide descriptive information about the respondent. Common demographic items on organizational surveys include items asking about gender, age, race or ethnicity, occupation, and education level.

To help decide what demographic information to collect, the survey team needs to think ahead to the specific analyses or breakouts it plans to do. For example, an organization conducting a diversity survey may be interested in the attitudes of subgroups broken down by race, gender, and age. Therefore, the survey team should include demographic items that assess these variables.

Although identifying the alternatives and questions used in gathering demographic information is relatively straightforward, this task should not be taken lightly. Improperly asked demographics can hamper later group comparisons. Archival sources such as U.S. Census Bureau reports are commonly used to derive demographic items. There are advantages to using Census Bureau or Bureau of Labor Statistics demographic items. First, the survey team is saved item development time. Second, these two governmental agencies have already field-tested the items using very large samples. Third, using the government's questions and alternatives allows an organization to compare findings obtained with its subgroups with statistics for similar subgroups in the population. Finally, if people complain about how certain demographic items such as race or ethnic status are worded (a particularly sensitive issue for many people), the survey team can respond, "Well it's not perfect, but that's the way the government asks those questions."

The survey should not include more demographic items than are truly needed, especially on an anonymous survey. If too many demographic data are requested, people may become suspicious about whether their answers are truly anonymous. Such suspicions can negatively affect the quality and truthfulness of the responses. This concern is heightened when the requested information is sensitive (e.g., alcohol abuse or employee theft). To reduce this problem, several authors (e.g., Frey, 1989; Miller, 1991) recommend that demographic items be placed at the end of the survey. This solution probably has limited positive effect for organizations that regularly survey their employees. Previously surveyed employees will know what's coming after the first time they see demographic items placed at the end of the survey.

Factual Items

Factual items ask for behavioral information or about other events within respondents' realm of experience. Some factual items ask for information, such as "How many jobs have you held in the past 10 years?" or "How many hours per week do you spend commuting to and from work?" Other factual items ask for information about the workplace, the job, or the organization. An example is "How many people (including yourself) are in your work group?"

The survey team should be aware that it may be difficult to get accurate factual information from respondents. The research literature is full of examples showing how inaccurate people are in reporting their behaviors and experiences (Tanur, 1992). The less salient and more routine the event or behavior is, the lower the accuracy of recall is likely to be. One recent study found that respondents recalled only 44% of their medical appointments within the prior year (Loftus, Smith, Klinger, & Fiedler, 1992). Thus, the team should not assume that people will be able to recall their behavior and experiences correctly over an extended period of time.[1]

There are some techniques for increasing the accurate reporting of factual information. These techniques include emphasizing to respondents that accuracy is important, explaining how the information will be used, providing respondents with lists of events or behaviors to aid recall, keeping the reference period short (e.g., within the past 6 months), and asking respondents to supply a date for each event or behavior (Tanur, 1992). Fowler (1993) provides additional guidelines for enhancing the quality of answers to factual questions.

Attitudinal Items

Attitudinal items ask for respondents' attitudes, opinions, beliefs, or perceptions on a topic. This type of item is very popular for organizational surveys. In part, this popularity stems from the fact that attitudinal items can be written on virtually every organization-related topic. Attitudinal items are used to determine how respondents perceive their jobs, bosses, coworkers, and various other aspects of work and the work setting. Attitudinal questions can present another organizational picture to supplement the one supplied by objective data.

Because attitudinal items often operate at the level of perceptions rather than facts or behaviors, they are sometimes criticized by action-oriented managers for being too soft and not relevant for specific organizational outcomes. Research (see Tedeschi, Lindskold, & Rosenfeld, 1985) has established, however, that attitudes are often related to later behavior. According to the *theory of reasoned action* (Ajzen & Fishbein, 1980), knowledge of a person's attitude toward a specific behavior as well as his or her perception of how others will evaluate the behavior (called the *subjective norm*) can lead to accurate predictions of a person's intentions to do the behavior. These behavioral intentions are usually related to subsequent actions. Attitudes can also affect behavior through the establishment of self-fulfilling prophecies. For example, if an employee feels that her supervisor has a negative attitude toward women, this may translate into her confirming the negative perception through poor work behaviors. It is important to include attitudinal items on organizational surveys so that managers can be made aware of any widespread negative perceptions and take corrective steps before these attitudes become manifested as negative behaviors (e.g., employee turnover, increased work absences, and poor productivity).

In some situations, attitudinal measures can be as important and as revealing as objective measures. This is particularly the case when the behavior or situation to be measured is a negative one (e.g., sexual harassment, employee theft). Negative behaviors and situations may be difficult to measure objectively because of their infrequency because employees generally do not engage in them openly and because of organizational policies and norms that prevent them from being reported.

Although it would be ideal to have both attitudinal and objective data on a topic, objective data are often impossible or impractical to obtain. Therefore, attitudinal measures may provide the best alternatives to objective measures.

Writing "Good" Items: Some Basic Rules

Writing survey items—whether closed ended, open ended, demographic, factual, or attitudinal—is an art rather than a science (Sheatsley, 1983). Creating well-written items involves more than using correct spelling and grammar. Constructing good items requires awareness of and adherence to some basic rules. Even those who know and follow the rules sometimes write bad or ambiguous items. The proof is often in the survey pretest, where the best-planned items may not turn out as expected. Dillman (1978) captures the frustration of a survey item writer who said, "Writing questions would be a lot easier if we did not have to use words!" (p. 75).

This section reviews rules that the survey team should follow when writing survey items. We must stress, however, that there is no perfect way to write an item. Differences in content, survey purpose, respondent comprehension level, and other factors can present exceptions to almost all the rules (Dillman, 1978). Still, an attempt to follow these rules takes the team a long way toward gathering better survey data.

Ask What You Want to Know

Among the most important rules for writing items is ask what you want to know, not something else (Bradburn & Sudman, 1988). Even experienced survey developers sometimes make the mistake of asking questions that cannot give them the information they need. When writing items, the survey team members should continually ask themselves, "Will the answers to this question tell us what we need to know?"

Keep Items Simple and Short

The KISS strategy—Keep it simple, stupid!—is good advice for survey item writers. The team should strive to write simple, clear items and to keep the items as short as possible (Converse & Presser, 1986; DeVellis, 1991; Spector, 1992). The longer the question, the more difficult the task of answering it is. When questions are long and cumbersome, respondents may forget the first part of the question by the time they get to the end (Alreck & Settle, 1985). Payne (1951) advocates using 25 or fewer words for an item, although other experts acknowledge that there is no magic number of words. There does seem to be a consensus that fewer words are better than more (Converse & Presser, 1986; Sheatsley, 1983).

Ask About Only One Topic per Item

One of the most common pitfalls is writing a survey item that asks about more than one topic or idea. Survey items that contain two separate ideas or try to combine two questions into one are called *double-barreled* (Alreck & Settle, 1985; DeVellis, 1991). Double-barreled items are common when an assessment is being made of two issues or topics that often go together in people's minds, such as salary and benefits.

The problem with double-barreled items is that agreement or disagreement with the item implies agreement or disagreement with both parts of it. Respondents who agree with one part (e.g., they are satisfied with their salary) and disagree with the other (e.g., they are dissatisfied with their benefits) are given no way to convey this viewpoint. The best way to deal with double-barreled items is to split the question into two or more items—one item per idea or topic. Separate items allow for the gathering of more precise and useful information.

Avoid Ambiguous or Vague Questions

When writing items, the team should keep in mind that the goal is to word each and every question so that all respondents interpret it in the same way. Although this goal is rarely achieved, it is worthwhile to strive to attain it.

When a question seems ambiguous to respondents, they may interpret the question as best they can and then answer the question in line with this interpretation rather than ask for clarification (Bradburn & Sudman, 1991). Different respondents could apply different interpretations to the same question. The more effort individuals must exert to determine the meaning of a question, the more uncertain the validity of their responses is (Berdie, Anderson, & Niebuhr, 1986). Vague or ambiguous questions are frustrating and may cause respondents to fail to complete all the survey items.

Questions may be ambiguous for a variety of reasons. A survey question may be ambiguous because it uses a vague term or phrase. For example, the question "Would you be willing to relocate?" is ambiguous because respondents presented with this question do not know precisely what relocation means (i.e., within the same city, within the state, out of state). Similarly, "Have you taken any drugs while at work in the past year?" is ambiguous because it is not clear whether drugs include prescriptions, over-the-counter medications, or illegal substances. Such questions can easily be improved by adding a phrase or statement defining the ambiguous term in question.

The team should look carefully at each question and ask itself if there is any alternative way that this question could be interpreted. When the team is satisfied with the questions, an additional and more decisive test for ambiguity can be achieved through a pretest. We have often been surprised that survey items that seemed crystal clear to us were regarded as ambiguous or unclear to our pretest respondents.

Use Appropriate Language

Questions should be worded at a level that is appropriate for the individuals who will complete the survey. Care needs to be exercised to avoid words or terms unfamiliar to those completing the survey. The sample to be surveyed may vary widely in education, literacy level, and background. What seems like a simple, straightforward question to the survey team can carry many different meanings to respondents who vary in life, work experiences, and education.

If the survey is designed for a specialized group, it is acceptable to use the jargon of that group, provided all respondents are familiar with it. For example, one of our students worked as a human resource management consultant in a sewage treatment factory. When he devised an employee attitude survey, it was entirely appropriate to include words such as "sludge" and other terms related to sewage treatment that were familiar to those who worked in the factory but may have been unclear to outsiders.

The best conceived organizational survey will fail if respondents do not understand what the items or instructions mean. Because the reading ability of the survey team is often higher than that of the average respondent, the team may incorrectly assume that all respondents will be able to read and understand the items (Sheatsley, 1983). For this reason, we recommend that the readability level of the survey items and directions be assessed. A *readability analysis* provides a score that suggests how easy or difficult it is to read and understand a passage. This analysis typically examines variables such as sentence and word length; whether simple, complex, or compound sentences are used; and the number of sentences per paragraph. Until recently, a readability analysis required special computer programs or hand scoring. Today, programs that work with standard word-processing software (e.g., Grammatik 5) can perform this analysis.

A readability analysis is not a substitute for a pretest in determining whether items and instructions are understood. Instead, it is an opportunity for the survey team to nip unneeded complexity in the bud, before the pretest. If the readability analysis shows that the reading level is too high (an earlier draft of this chapter was at the 21st grade level!), the problem can be resolved before the pretest.

A high school diploma does not guarantee that someone reads at a 12th grade level. If your workforce consists entirely of high school graduates, it is best to aim for a readability level below 12th grade. In general, keeping the readability level below the reading level of the average organizational member increases the likelihood that all respondents will understand the intended meaning of survey items.

Be Specific

Specific items are usually better than general items because they are associated with more accurate recall, are likely to be interpreted similarly by all respondents, and predict future behavior better (Converse & Presser, 1986). Futrell (1994) suggests that the best way to avoid nonspecific questions on organizational surveys is to look at each question and ask, "If we get a poor rating on this question, will we know what needs to be fixed?" A "No" answer means that the item should be rewritten because it is too general to yield a specific course of action.

The problem with a general item such as "How satisfied are you with the company health plan?" is that responses provide little information if change is needed. A series of specific items eliciting ratings for different aspects of the health plan would be better. Table 3.1 shows some of the

TABLE 3.1 Example Illustrating the Use of Specific Items

Use the following satisfaction scale to indicate how satisfied or dissatisfied you are with the following aspects of the company health plan.

(1) Very dissatisfied	(2) Dissatisfied	(3) Neither satisfied nor dissatisfied	(4) Satisfied	(5) Very satisfied

_____ a. Cost of the policy

_____ b. Co-payment costs for services

_____ c. Co-payment costs for medicine

_____ d. Availability of physicians

_____ e. Types of services covered by the policy

_____ f. Amount of paperwork required when filing a claim

specific items that might be included in an assessment of members' satisfaction with the organization's health plan. Besides providing more specific information, responses to the individual items can be used to form a *summated scale score*—the sum of ratings on all items assessing the same topic—that portrays respondents' overall satisfaction.

Double Negatives: NOT!

Except in rare instances, double negatives are definitely a survey no-no. A double-negative item may ask respondents to disagree that something is false or negative. This situation results in "an awkward statement and a potential source of considerable error" (Sheatsley, 1983, p. 217). An organizational example of a double negative is, "I do not support the idea of not allowing employees to work back-to-back shifts." Items with double negatives are confusing and difficult. Some respondents will fail to notice that there are two negatives in the question and will give an answer opposite in meaning to the one they really intended to give. For this reason, items containing double negatives should be reworded or eliminated.

Avoid Biased Items

In a survey conducted by the National Opinion Research Center, individuals were asked if the United States was spending too much, too little, or about the right amount of money on "assistance to the poor." About two thirds of respondents indicated that the country was spending too little. When "assistance to the poor" was changed to "welfare," about half the respondents said that too much was being spent on welfare (Kagay & Elder, 1992). This example illustrates how easily bias can be introduced into a survey answer by seemingly very similar questions.

Many times, bias is in the form of a leading question. In leading questions, the phrasing of the question nudges the survey responses in one direction or the other. An example of a leading question is, "Most people feel that training is extremely important for career advancement. Do you agree?" Few would feel comfortable disagreeing with this question, especially after being told that they are going to hold an opinion different from most other people.

Leading questions are sometimes used deliberately to achieve personal goals. For example, a training director might be in charge of giving a survey to evaluate the effectiveness of a new management course. There could be pressure on the director to show that the course was worth the organization's investment. As a result, the director might be tempted to write the questions so that the trainees will respond favorably. Respondents would have little opportunity to express weaknesses with the training course if they were asked questions such as "In what ways did this course increase your knowledge of sound management principles?" and "How will the knowledge you got from this course help you do your job better?"

Some survey developers write leading questions without being aware of it (Fink & Kosecoff, 1985). Consequently, it is a good idea to have an outside party examine the items before the survey goes out. The pretest can also be used to catch leading questions. The point is that what seems neutral to the survey team may seem biased to some respondents.

Take Care With Sensitive Items

Asking sensitive questions on surveys has always been a difficult issue. People vary greatly in the amount and type of information they are willing to disclose about themselves. For example, many people resent being asked questions about their salary, race, or ethnic status. On our diversity surveys, race and ethnic status are assessed using two separate items. One question asks about race (e.g., white, African American) and a second one asks whether the respondent is of Hispanic origin (because Hispanics can be members of any racial group). Despite the fact that the U.S. Census Bureau has assessed Hispanic origin in this fashion, some respondents complained because they thought Hispanics were being negatively singled out. Other respondents complained because they felt the survey gave Hispanics too much attention! The best way to find out whether a survey contains any sensitive items is to pretest the survey on a small sample similar to the group that will eventually receive the instrument. Individuals who find a question sensitive or objectionable may be able to suggest a better way to gather the same or similar data in a manner that would raise fewer caution flags.

Questions about drug and alcohol usage, unauthorized work-related actions (e.g., playing computer games on work time), and illegal behaviors (e.g., employee theft) are regarded as sensitive by most people. If the sensitive information is not truly needed, these questions should be omitted. If there is truly a need for this sensitive information, care should be taken in the wording and placement of the items. When asking about embarrassing or illegal behaviors, preface the question with a statement that makes it less embarrassing for respondents to admit to the behavior. For drug use, this type of phrasing might result in the following item: "People have many different reasons for taking illegal drugs. In the past year, have you used any illegal drugs while at work?" To minimize the potential negative effects of sensitive items, a number of survey experts (e.g., Bradburn & Sudman, 1991) suggest that such items should be put toward the end of the questionnaire.

Another way of obtaining sensitive data is to ask for the information using general multiple-choice categories. When asking questions about income (a topic that many people find highly sensitive), Dillman (1978) suggests that it is best to use a series of broad categories (e.g., $10,000 to $25,000; $25,001 to $40,000) rather than asking people to list their exact annual income. This same approach can be used for other sensitive content areas.

A recent General Accounting Office (1993) publication suggests some useful guidelines for asking sensitive survey questions. These include explaining the reason for asking the sensitive questions, explaining how the information will be used, making sure respondents know that the sensitive information will not be used in a threatening way, wording the questions in a nonjudgmental way, portraying the behavior as socially acceptable, and guaranteeing anonymity and confidentiality when possible. Box 3.1 explores additional aspects of issues relating to anonymity and confidentiality in organizational surveys.

BOX 3.1

Anonymity and Confidentiality on Organizational Surveys

Organizational surveys often ask respondents sensitive questions about their supervisors, coworkers, working conditions, and turnover intentions. It is obvious that, in many situations, revealing respondents' survey answers to these and other sensitive questions could cause respondents harm or result in reprisal. Also, if respondents even suspect that others in the organization might be able to associate them with their survey responses (a common fear, in our experience), their responses will be less candid. They may say what they perceive to be the right thing rather than what they truly believe. In most cases, survey teams can protect respondents from potential harm and improve the candidness of survey responses by providing anonymity or confidentiality.

Survey responses are typically solicited along a continuum that varies from fully anonymous to fully identi-

fied, with confidential being somewhere between these extremes. A survey is anonymous when the respondent simply supplies the requested survey data without any personal identifiers. In an anonymous survey neither the person administering the survey nor anyone else in the organization can link an individual to his or her responses. A mail-back survey that does not contain the respondent's name, identification numbers, or identifying information (e.g., demographics) provides a high level of anonymity.

On an identified survey, respondents can be linked to their answers as a result of having provided their names or other identifying information such as social security number. Surveys that attempt to track the same respondents over time often ask for such identifying information. A survey is confidential when the survey team agrees not to give anyone else access to the respondent's survey data. Both identified and anonymous survey information can be confidential if access to the data and actual surveys are limited to the members of the team.

While complete anonymity and confidentiality provide respondents with the greatest protection from intentional or accidental harm, there are several factors that determine the degree to which anonymity or confidentiality is desirable or possible. These factors include the survey administration method, the reason(s) for the survey, the survey context, and the degree to which survey responses are grouped when analyzed and presented. For example, confidentiality may be possible in telephone and face-to-face interview surveys, but complete anonymity is probably not possible for either of these administration methods.

Most people who complete organizational surveys prefer to be anonymous if they are divulging sensitive information (e.g., opinions about their supervisor or the likelihood of quitting in the next year). In contrast, the same workers would probably not be reluctant to complete an identified survey that asked about the quality of the food in the cafeteria.

The way the data are aggregated for analysis and presentation also may impact on anonymity. Suppose there were only five women who completed a sexual harassment survey in the supply department of a large company. If high levels of harassment by supervisors were reported by these women, a vindictive manager might retaliate in some way, given that he knows who these five people were. It would be even worse if other demographic breakdowns (e.g., race, job type) were available for this already small number of people. For this reason, we and most professional survey organizations refuse to report the means, frequencies, or other statistics for groups smaller than 10 people (Scarpello & Vandenberg, 1991). We also take care that output from statistical programs containing such small group breakouts is not distributed and does not circulate outside of the survey team.[2]

The survey team should clearly convey through written and/or oral instructions the survey's level of anonymity and confidentiality and, if necessary, why identification is required. If anonymity and confidentiality are not guaranteed, the survey instructions should warn respondents that, for example, their answers may be provided to others exactly as the answers are written. If a member of the team reneges after promising anonymity or confidentiality, serious damage could result to all future surveys in that organization. For practical, ethical, and legal reasons, the survey team must consider this issue carefully and make sure that respondents understand how anonymous or confidential their answers will be (Sieber, 1992).

Granting anonymity and confidentiality often leads to two significant benefits. A higher proportion of the surveys will likely be returned if the surveys are completed anonymously than if they are completed under identified conditions. The other major benefit is that anonymity often results in more candid responses than answers given when respondents are identified (Booth-Kewley, Edwards, & Rosenfeld, 1992).

A disadvantage of anonymity is that it prevents linking a person's answers to other databases such as those containing information on training, job experience, and test scores (i.e., aptitude, achievement, or vocational). Similarly, anonymity makes it more difficult to tie a person's answers on Survey 1 to the same person's answers on Survey 2 that is administered later. This constraint may limit the survey team to cross-sectional rather than longitudinal designs for assessing changes.

One of the reviewers for this book suggested an alternative that might be useful for overcoming the problem of doing longitudinal research with anonymous surveys (especially for surveys that have smaller numbers of respondents). The problem of linking two surveys completed by the same person at two points in time can be circumvented by asking respondents to create their own identification code known only to them. They might be asked, for example, to create a code using information from their mother's maiden name, the street address where they lived at age 13, and their father's middle name. Two rounds of surveys could thereby be linked with this code.

Alternatively, the survey team could administer a survey that includes embedded identification codes. These are codes that are printed on the survey and can be scanned at a later time to see which respondents returned the survey. Using embedded codes on a mail-out survey allows the team to send follow-up surveys just to those who did not return the survey rather than to everyone. By using a code rather than a name, the chances of a person being directly linked to his or her answers (intentionally or accidentally) are reduced. ZX309-134 may be meaningful to a scanner, but it is unlikely that a supervisor or coworker could match it to an employee's name if the team is careful about protecting the codes. If this step is taken, the survey team is ethically bound to inform potential respondents about the presence and purposes of the codes.

Conclusions

This chapter has presented the advantages and disadvantages of open- and closed-ended item formats; reviewed the use of demographic, factual, and attitudinal questions; and provided basic rules for writing good items. Although the rules may not be appropriate for every item, adherence to the rules should provide the survey team with easily understood items that accurately assess desired content areas.

Notes

1. Routine behaviors are reported more accurately if the behavior has a regular pattern (e.g., drinking a cup of coffee every morning) and occurs at only one specific time.

2. Although 10 is often used as the minimum number for breakouts, there is nothing magical about that number. Indeed, if negative information is involved, potential harm can be caused by almost any small group breakout. For example, if a survey indicates that 15 (30%) of the 50 employees in the supply department admit to having taken drugs or alcohol while on the job, this may cause management to become suspicious of everyone in the supply department.

Creating the Survey, Part II

Response Alternatives, Item Order, Survey Length, and Response Biases

4

In addition to the items themselves, the quality of an organizational survey instrument depends on factors such as how response alternatives are presented, item order, and survey length. Respondent characteristics also come into play in the form of response biases. This chapter reviews these areas and offers suggestions for improving the survey team's chances of obtaining reliable and valid data.

Getting Good Answers: Choosing Closed-Ended Response Formats

No matter how good the first part or stem of a closed-ended item is, survey responses will be of dubious validity if the response alternatives are not adequate. Incomplete, overlapping, inappropriate, or vague response options frustrate respondents and lead to unreliable responses. Moreover, respondents often use the response options as guides for interpreting a question and as cues for determining the appropriateness of their responses. Therefore, as much care should be taken in developing and displaying response options as goes into the writing of the item.

Multiple-Choice Response Format

Most, if not all, surveys include items that use the multiple-choice response format. With this type of item, respondents are asked to pick one or more answers from a list of alternatives. An item assessing the gender of respondents would have two choices: Male or Female. Another example of this format is, "In which department do you currently work?"; this stem is followed by a list of all possible departments in the organization.

Items that use multiple-choice response options include demographic items (e.g., income category and marital status) and other questions asking for qualitative information (e.g., job type and department). Typically, the number of response alternatives ranges from two to six. The number of alternatives depends on how broad or specific the listed options are. This, in turn, depends on how fine-grained the information needs to be. If many narrow alternatives are provided, the respondents' burden is increased and statistical processing takes more time. If, however, the survey team honestly believes that more specific information would be useful, a list of specific categories should be used. When in doubt, the survey team should opt for fine-grained alternatives because the specific answers can be regrouped later into more general categories, but the opposite is not true.

▨ *Marking One or Multiple Alternatives From a List*

The instructions for multiple-choice items usually tell the respondents to select the one alternative that is most descriptive. Less frequently, respondents are instructed to mark or check all the answers that apply. An example of this kind of item is:

> During the past 12 months, which of the following company-sponsored training programs have you attended? (Check all that apply)
>
> ____(a) Computer training
>
> ____(b) Sexual harassment training
>
> ____(c) Supervisory skills seminar
>
> ____(d) Stress management workshop
>
> ____(e) Not applicable. I did not attend training in the past 12 months.

We sparingly use multiple-choice items that allow more than one alternative to be marked. Asking respondents to switch between mark-all-that-apply items and single-response items is confusing. The result may be the respondent's choosing too many or too few of the alternatives or not marking any alternative.

▨ *Exhaustive and Mutually Exclusive Responses*

It is more difficult to develop response options for multiple-choice items than for any other type of survey item. The primary reason for this difficulty is the need to identify and list all potential answers. If the question "In which department do you currently work?" is followed by a list that includes only the eight largest departments in the organization, respondents who work for other departments will be puzzled as to how they should respond. As a result, they might leave the item blank or they might incorrectly select one of the listed departments. Therefore, it is very important that multiple-choice response alternatives be exhaustive. That is, every effort must be made to identify all potential response categories.

Response options should not overlap; they should be mutually exclusive. Overlap causes confusion about which option to select. An engineer who is also a manager would not be able to answer the following question correctly and fully:

> What is your occupation? (Check one)
>
> ____(a) Accounting
>
> ____(b) Clerical

_____(c) Engineering

_____(d) Management

_____(e) Marketing

_____(f) Production

_____(g) Sales

_____(h) Other

The employee's profession and organizational level are not mutually exclusive categories, and both issues are related to the individual's occupation.

In these situations, some respondents may choose multiple alternatives even when they have been instructed to select only one. This item could be improved by changing it to a mark-all-that-apply question or by separating the profession alternatives from the organizational level choices. That is, respondents could be asked in one question whether or not they are managers. A second question could then be used to inquire about the respondents' profession.

The list should be presented in a logical order. For example, the above list was presented in alphabetical order. Alternatives might be ordered according to time or the anticipated frequency of the alternatives. If the order of response options is not logical, the response quality is likely to be diminished.

The survey team needs to be especially careful to ensure that alternatives are mutually exclusive when asking about time and frequency. For example, one of us recently critiqued a survey that had the item "How often do you file program updates?"; the response alternatives were "at least once a day," "several times per week," and "several times per month." The alternatives are not mutually exclusive because the day alternative fits within the week alternative and both of those alternatives could fit within the several-times-per-month alternative.

▧ *Special Alternatives:*
Other (Please Specify),
Don't Know, and Not
Applicable

Many times, the survey team knows that a question is needed, but the focus group interviews did not identify an exhaustive list of alternatives. What can the survey team do to avoid using a open-ended question? One solution is to list the response categories that were identified and then add the alternative "Other (Please specify)." If the respondent finds that none of the alternatives fits, that person marks the space beside the "Other (Please specify)" alternative and writes a brief narrative answer. Because the survey team will need to code each narrative response before it is entered into the computer, every effort should be made to avoid this by identifying an exhaustive list.

At other times, survey developers include the "Don't know" response option as part of a multiple-choice list. The major advantage of including this alternative is that the respondent is provided an out if she or he is not familiar with the issue, has not had the experience in question, or does not understand the item. Forcing respondents to provide an answer about a topic with which they are unfamiliar adds measurement error to the results. Although there is no consensus in the survey literature on whether a "Don't know" alternative should be presented, we believe it is appropriate for items in which there is a real chance that some respondents will be unable to answer the question.

Depending on the content of the survey items, it is also often appropriate to include "Not applicable" as a response alternative. If questions are irrelevant for some respondents (e.g., questions about the quality of on-site child care for respondents without children), those respondents should be allowed either to indicate that the question is irrelevant for them or to skip the question.

When only one or two items are irrelevant, we prefer to provide a "Not applicable" alternative for each question. When a whole section of items is irrelevant for a subgroup of respondents, those respondents should be told to skip or branch to a later section without reading and answering the nonpertinent items. That instruction can be made as part of a response alternative or as a general instruction that follows the question and alternatives.

A cautionary note is needed about the use of *skip patterns*. If respondents are told to skip questions that do not apply to them, some respondents will skip questions inappropriately. One study (Messmer & Seymour, 1982) found that skipping (also called *item branching*) instructions significantly increased the rate of item nonresponse for items following skip patterns. When branching increases the level of blank responses, it is difficult or impossible (during analyses) to determine which questions were skipped because they did not apply and which items were left blank for other reasons.

Yes-No and True-False Response Formats

These two response formats are variations of the multiple-choice format. In both cases, the two response alternatives may be followed by a third option—"Don't know" or "Not applicable." These response formats are primarily used to gather data of a factual nature from items, such as "Have you received a promotion in the past 12 months?"

The appeal of these formats results from their simplicity of use, processing, analysis, and presentation. We have found that action-oriented managers really like these formats, especially when the findings are presented in a simple and easy-to-understand manner indicating the percentage of people who marked "Yes" or "No" (or "True" or "False"). Spector (1992) notes that this advantage sometimes comes at a price. The use of only two response categories makes it difficult to measure complex issues with precision or to assess differences in intensity. In such cases, the survey team may be better served by using rating scales to measure the degree to which something is true or not.

Likert Rating Scales

The most widely used response format is the *rating scale,* with the Likert scale being the most popular form. On Likert rating scales, survey respondents are asked to provide ratings indicating how strongly they feel positively or negatively on an issue. A set of Likert-scale items is shown in Table 4.1.

In Table 4.1, respondents are asked to indicate the amount to which they agree or disagree with a variety of statements. Although agree-disagree alternatives are used primarily to gather attitudinal data, Likert scales that use other words to anchor the numerical ratings provide added flexibility for gathering other types of information. Table 4.2 gives additional sets of anchors that can be used with Likert-type items.

Gathering and processing Likert-type responses are efficient. Respondents know how to complete Likert items because nearly everyone has, at one time or another, been asked to rate something using a Likert scale (even though they did not know the technical name of the rating format). Using the same response alternatives for numerous items allows respondents to supply a large amount of information in a small amount of time. Furthermore, rating scales have the advantage of providing data that use values rather than merely categories. This provides much greater flexibility during the later analysis phase.

▨ *How Many Points Should a Rating Scale Have?*

Although the Likert format can have any number of points, most surveys employ scales using 5 to 11 points (Bradburn & Sudman, 1991). Use of a greater number of points does not enhance measurement because respondents are unable to make such fine distinctions (Bradburn & Sudman,

---

TABLE 4.1 The Likert Response Format

Use the following scale to indicate how much you agree or disagree with the following statements.

(1) *Strongly* *disagree*	*(2)* *Disagree*	*(3)* *Neither agree* *nor disagree*	*(4)* *Agree*	*(5)* *Strongly* *agree*

_____ My boss makes me feel like a valued employee.

_____ My boss is unreasonable.

_____ I respect my boss.

_____ I feel comfortable talking to my boss about work-related problems.

TABLE 4.2 Examples of Response Formats Used in Opinion and Attitude Surveys

	Points Along the Scale Continuum				
Type of Scale	*1*	*2*	*3*	*4*	*5*
Agreement	Strongly disagree	Disagree	Neither agree nor disagree	Agree	Strongly agree
Satisfaction	Very dissatisfied	Dissatisfied	Neither satisfied nor dissatisfied	Satisfied	Very satisfied
Frequency	Never	Seldom	About half the time	Often	Always
Effectiveness	Very ineffective	Ineffective	Neither effective nor ineffective	Effective	Very effective
Quality	Very poor	Poor	Average	Good	Very good
Expectancy	Much worse than expected	Worse than expected	As expected	Better than expected	Much better than expected
Extent	To no extent	To a small extent	To a moderate extent	To a great extent	To a very great extent

1991). Regardless of how many points are used, it is important to include rating-scale anchors or labels (e.g., "Strongly disagree") that correspond to the numerical points on the scale (Paul & Bracken, 1995). Identifying meaningful anchor labels is obviously easier when fewer points are used.

▥ *Should a Scale Have a Midpoint?*

One controversial issue in the use of Likert scales is whether the rating scale should contain a neutral point or midpoint (Schwarz & Hippler, 1991). Under most circumstances, we use midpoints. There are at least three reasons for our decision. First, including a midpoint is the only way to allow respondents who truly hold a neutral attitude to express accurately how they feel or think. Eliminating the midpoint would add measurement error by forcing all the neutral respondents to choose options that do not reflect their true feelings. Second, respondents may find it frustrating to be forced into expressing an opinion when they feel neutral or ambivalent on the topic. Causing too much frustration might result in the respondent's opting not to return a survey. Third, when computing averages for the survey items or dimensions, some of the means will invariably have values at the midpoint of the scale. It is awkward to discuss results falling at the midpoint when the survey items themselves did not include a midpoint option.

The experience of one of us illustrates that problems can also result when a midpoint is used on an organizational survey. Years ago, the young, aspiring author-researcher presented results from an employee opinion survey to the personnel director of a large organization. On many of the survey items, up to 40% of the respondents chose the midpoint ("Neither agree nor disagree") as their answer. It was very difficult to interpret the meaning of these midpoint responses. Because of this, the action-oriented personnel director was dissatisfied with the survey findings. The director demanded to know whether midpoint responses could be interpreted as good or bad. The rapidly aging researcher had to use the "Don't know" option as his response to the director!

This example illustrates why some survey developers prefer to force respondents to choose one side or the other of the continuum and, therefore, do not supply a scale midpoint.

Because the debate on the use of a midpoint has a long history with no definitive conclusion (see Converse & Presser, 1986; DeVellis, 1991; Schuman & Presser, 1981), we will not attempt to settle the controversy here. Instead, the survey team should do whatever is appropriate given the content matter being assessed, the respondent population, and organizational preferences. The survey team should derive some comfort knowing that there are strong reasons supporting the inclusion or the exclusion of a midpoint.

■ *Combining Items Into Dimensions*

The response to any single closed-ended item on a survey may not be an accurate indicator about what people feel about a topic. One testing expert (Nunnally, 1967) states that the correlation is typically .40 or below between the answer to a single item and the total score for all items measuring the same characteristic. The problem with using a single item to measure a particular characteristic is that the one item is likely to be fairly unreliable. Any single item may be ambiguous, contain confusing language, or mean different things to different people. Because of these concerns, survey professionals often group responses from several items together. This grouping of items is referred to as a *dimension,* an *index,* or a *scale* (Converse & Presser, 1986).[1]

Multi-item dimensions (e.g., job satisfaction, work motivation, and task ambiguity) are collections of individual questions combined to enhance the measurement of a characteristic. Items included in the same dimension should have a strong relationship to the characteristic they are supposed to measure, and the items should be logically related to each other (DeVellis, 1991). For example, the dimension of organizational climate might include the following items: "I feel a strong sense of loyalty to this organization," "I have no plans to leave this organization," "I am willing to put myself out to help this organization," and "I am strongly committed to this organization." The respondent's dimension score is usually either the sum or the average of responses to the individual items.

Four major advantages result from using multiple items rather than a single question to assess a dimension. First, a multi-item dimension score typically gives a more reliable indication of the person's overall views on a topic than does a single-item dimension score. Second, combining individual items into a dimension allows each respondent to be assigned a single dimension score. A multi-item variable or dimension is easier and more succinctly presented than are separate (and possibly conflicting) findings for each item. Third, the degree to which respondents possess a characteristic can be distinguished more finely with a multi-item dimension score. Fourth, the survey team can drop a "bad" item and still have an index measuring the characteristic of interest.

These advantages are balanced by disadvantages. Some characteristics are so narrowly defined that it is difficult to write more than one or two items to assess the characteristic. Also, answering each additional item requires a proportionally larger amount of respondent time. If there are many multi-item dimensions, the result could be a very long survey.

Thurstone Scaling

Thurstone scales are more complex than Likert scales. Several steps are required to arrive at a series of statements—each with its own weight or value. Miller (1991) provides an overview of the steps used in this procedure. To develop an instrument to measure, say, job satisfaction, the survey team writes a large number of job satisfaction items. Next, the survey team has subject matter experts classify each statement into 1 of 11 categories of favorableness or unfavorableness. Third, the survey team computes a mean (or median) rating and assigns the value to the statement. Statements are discarded if the assignment of the statement is variable across experts. The Thurstone scale is then formed by selecting statements evenly spread from one extreme to the other (i.e., 1 to 11). Table 4.3 shows an example of a 4-item Thurstone scale that might be used on an organizational survey. Although the numbers in parentheses are not provided to respondents, they indicate the Thurstone values assigned to each item.

When answering Thurstone items, respondents are told to choose the items (e.g., two) most descriptive of their opinions, feelings, and the like. A respondent's score on the dimension is the average of the Thurstone-scaled values for the selected items.

Although it played an important role in the history of attitude measurement (see Tedeschi et al., 1985), the Thurstone format is rarely used today in organizational surveys. The labor intensiveness of the dimension construction process and the need for a large number of experts to do the item rating and sorting are often impractical and too expensive.

Semantic Differential Scaling

In a *semantic differential scaling,* people judge a particular concept or issue using a set of scales anchored at their extreme points by words of opposite meaning. Typically, the word pairs are adjectives (e.g., "Good-Bad," "Relaxed-Tense," and "Helpful-Harmful") and the number of scale points

TABLE 4.3 An Example of Thurstone Scaling

Place a check mark beside the statement that best describes how much pressure/stress that you feel at work.

_____ It is rare for me to feel pressured at work. (1.4)

_____ My job is occasionally stressful. (3.8)

_____ I often feel under pressure at work. (7.3)

_____ The amount of stress that I experience at work is enormous. (10.7)

TABLE 4.4 An Example of Semantic Differential Scaling

Please tell us how you feel about your interactions with your supervisor. On each line, place a check mark between each pair of adjectives. The check mark should be placed toward the middle if you have neutral feelings about those interactions or toward one of the extremes if one of the words describes your interactions.

Helpful	___ ___ ___ ___ ___ ___ ___	Harmful
Too frequent	___ ___ ___ ___ ___ ___ ___	Too infrequent
Too short	___ ___ ___ ___ ___ ___ ___	Too long
Relaxed	___ ___ ___ ___ ___ ___ ___	Tense
Good	___ ___ ___ ___ ___ ___ ___	Bad
Wasteful	___ ___ ___ ___ ___ ___ ___	Useful

is between 5 and 11. To develop a set of semantic differential items, the survey team decides on the characteristics it wants to assess. Then it identifies adjectives descriptive of the characteristic and their opposites. Table 4.4 provides an example of a hypothetical 6-item semantic differential scale assessing interactions with one's supervisor.

To complete semantic differential scales, respondents mark the place on the scale that best describes their perceptions, attitudes, and the like. The results of semantic differential scales can be used to assess respondents' overall perceptions of different concepts or issues. Although we have occasionally used this rating format, we more often choose Likert-type scales on our organizational surveys.

Response Biases: The Downside of Using Closed-Ended Items

In the prior section, rules and guidelines were provided to facilitate the construction of clear, easily understood, closed-ended items. At the same time the survey team is writing items, it needs to be aware of the various biases that can affect how respondents answer closed-ended questions. A *response bias* is a tendency to respond in certain ways regardless of a question's content. It occurs when an answer to an item partially or wholly reflects an extraneous characteristic of the respondent or survey, rather than the respondent's true feelings, knowledge, or perceptions about an issue. This section identifies some of the more common response biases, defines them, and suggests steps that the survey team can take to minimize their effects.

Response Order Effects

Response order effects occur on items that supply respondents with a list of alternatives from which to choose an answer (i.e., multiple-choice, Yes-No, and True-False). There are two major response order effects: primacy and recency. A *primacy effect* is the tendency to remember better and, therefore, to choose an initial alternative from a list. A primacy effect might also occur because a respondent stops reading alternatives once he or she encounters an option that he or she minimally agrees with. A *recency effect* occurs when the last alternative is more likely to be remembered and chosen. If the list of alternatives is long, a respondent might better remember and select a more recently presented alternative (rather than the best alternative).

The occurrence of response order effects is related to survey administration method (Ayidiya & McClendon, 1990). Recency effects occur much more frequently than primacy effects when the alternatives are presented orally in interviews. Primacy effects occur more frequently when surveys are self-administered or when interviewees are able to read the answers themselves (rather than having the answers read to them) before selecting a response. To reduce the effect of response order effects, it is recommended that (a) lists of response alternatives be short, (b) lists be presented in writing rather than orally, and (c) each alternative on the list be evaluated on a rating scale rather than having the respondent choose one alternative over the other (Alreck & Settle, 1985).

Yea-Saying or Nay-Saying

Yea-saying or *nay-saying* bias is a tendency to agree or disagree with survey items regardless of their content (DeVellis, 1991; Oskamp, 1991). At its worst, a respondent may draw a line through one answer column to indicate that the same answer applies throughout (Paul & Bracken, 1995). In such cases, it might even be questioned whether the respondent took the time to read the items.

If numerous respondents are chronic yea-sayers and the survey items are all positively stated (e.g., "I plan to stay with this organization until retirement" and "My supervisor gives me feedback on my performance"), organizational problems such as employee dissatisfaction can be underestimated. Conversely, respondents who blindly agree with negatively stated items (e.g., "My supervisor rarely provides me with career counseling") might lead the survey team to conclude that a higher level of organizational dysfunction exists than is actually the case.

A popular technique for reducing the effect of yea-saying and nay-saying is to include both positively and negatively worded items when measuring a particular survey topic area (Edwards & Thomas, 1993). This procedure has been called the *balanced-scale approach* (Oskamp, 1991). It is assumed that yea-saying or nay-saying will be minimized by forcing respondents to read the items more carefully and use both ends of a rating scale.

Although this process may reduce the bias caused by the tendency to agree or disagree indiscriminately with items regardless of content, it raises other concerns. If both positively and negatively worded items are used to measure a single dimension and the survey team wishes to calculate a dimension mean or total score for each respondent, the responses for the negatively worded items must be reverse-scored (e.g., on a 5-point scale, 1 equals 5, 4 equals 2) before they can be added to the ratings for the positively worded items (Paul & Bracken, 1995).

More important, a negative answer (e.g., disagreement or disapproval) to a negatively worded statement may not be equivalent to a positive answer to a positively worded statement. For example, disagreeing with the statement "My work is not meaningful" does not necessarily mean that the same respondent would have agreed with the same intensity to the statement "My work is meaningful." Finally, respondents may find switching between positively and negatively worded items confusing (DeVellis, 1991). Failure to notice such switches results in inaccurate data. Such a problem is less common for individuals who are better educated and come from higher socioeconomic groups (Oskamp, 1991). Therefore, the decision to use balanced items may depend on the characteristics of the population being surveyed.

Acquiescence

In *acquiescence,* respondents give answers based on what they think the survey team or the sponsor of the survey wants to hear (Alreck & Settle, 1985). For example, if respondents believe that the survey team wants them to say positive things about the organization, the respondents may answer the items about the organization in an overly positive way. Acquiescence can be minimized by conveying to the respondents at the beginning of the survey that their honest, accurate input is needed and that there are no right or wrong answers. In addition, the survey team should word questions so that respondents cannot readily determine which answers are expected or desired.

Socially Desirable Responding

Responses on organizational surveys may be biased by the tendency of people to give socially appropriate answers rather than indicating what they really believe. This tendency to fake or say the right thing rather than give a candid response is known as *socially desirable responding* (Fowler,

1993; Oskamp, 1991; Spector, 1992). For example, in response to survey items, a bigot indicates he supports affirmative action, a chain smoker says that she smokes only a few cigarettes a day, and a perpetually tardy employee asserts that he almost always shows up for work on time. It is common for people to give socially desirable answers to questions about voting, donating to charity, abusing drugs or alcohol, and behaving unethically. Survey respondents who commit this type of response bias stretch the truth to make a good impression (Martin & Nagao, 1989).

One way of reducing situational pressure to respond in a socially desirable manner is to use *demand reduction techniques* (Paulhus, 1991). Common demand reduction techniques include stressing that the organizational survey responses are anonymous or confidential, using survey instructions to emphasize the importance of accurate responses, and minimizing the judgmental nature of the survey by indicating that there are no right or wrong answers (Fowler, 1993; Oskamp, 1991).

How Many Survey Items?

Once mastery of the basic rules of writing items and choosing response alternatives has been attained, the temptation may be to write a lot of items—more than necessary. If there are many cooks in the survey kitchen, the tendency may be to include everyone's favorite items in the spirit of compromise. This solution avoids the risk of offending coworkers or managers by eliminating their pet questions. But less is often better in the survey business. For financial, logistical, and methodological reasons, it is a good idea to limit the number of items that appear in the final version of the survey.

One of the first questions that aspiring survey writers ask is "How many items should my survey have?" In our informal poll of survey practices for the San Diego area, about two thirds of the respondents said that their typical organizational survey was 50 items or fewer. Paul and Bracken (1995) suggest that 80 to 100 items (excluding demographics) and a completion time of about 30 minutes are appropriate for most employee surveys. In contrast to these estimates, one of our recent organizational surveys had about 300 items.

There is no ideal length as measured by number of items, number of pages, or survey completion time. As an old cigarette advertisement said, "It's not how long you make it, it's how you make it long!" The survey team must balance a variety of sometimes conflicting considerations in determining survey length. Several of the more important concerns are listed below.

What Are the Goals of the Survey?

If a goal of the survey is to assess opinions on a large number of different issues, the survey will be longer than a survey that addresses only one or two specific issues. Also, if a goal of the survey is to obtain an in-depth understanding of respondents' behaviors and attitudes regarding an issue (e.g., employee wellness programs), the survey will be much longer than a questionnaire that is simply trying to determine the frequency of some behavior or experience (e.g., the number of individuals who have used employee wellness programs in the past year).

How Much Is the Company Willing to Pay?

The survey team should not forget that long surveys cost more than short surveys. Longer surveys incur greater paper, printing, and mailing costs (if a mail survey); often have lower response rates; and involve more time for coding, entering, and analyzing data. Longer surveys also take more time for the respondents to complete. This time translates into lost labor hours because most organizational surveys are completed on company time.

Who Will Complete the Questionnaire?

Some authors (Paul & Bracken, 1995; Scarpello & Vandenberg, 1991) note that managers prefer shorter surveys (3 to 5 pages), whereas nonmanagers prefer longer instruments (10 to 12 pages). Respondents who are allowed to fill out the survey on company time may be more tolerant of longer surveys than those who are expected to complete the survey at home (e.g., college alumni) or in the office of another company (e.g., respondents to a customer satisfaction survey). Also, individuals who do not enjoy reading or writing and who routinely avoid such activities may be very resistant to long surveys.

The education level of the respondents might be another factor influencing the number of items. On average, people attaining higher levels of education will probably be able to complete the survey faster than respondents with less education.

Are the Items Open or Closed Ended?

Open-ended questions take longer to complete than most closed-ended questions. If the survey is being completed on company time, there will often be a limited amount of time that employees are allowed to be away from their work spaces. Thus, when time available to complete the survey is a half hour or less, it is a good idea not to include too many open-ended items. For example, if the survey team has been given 20 minutes for each respondent to complete the survey, using even one or two open-ended questions might severely limit the number of closed-ended items that can be included on the survey.

What Is the Administration Method?

Because an interview survey generally takes much longer than a self-administered survey, fewer items can be included given that a fixed amount of time (e.g., 1 hour) is usually allotted for each respondent to complete the survey. Computer administered surveys take less time than equivalent paper surveys when numerous skip patterns are involved.

How Fast Are Data Needed?

If the results of the survey are needed quickly, the survey should be kept short. If more time is available, a longer, more in-depth survey may be appropriate. Regardless of how good and in-depth a survey is, it is of limited use if the findings arrive too late (Sheatsley, 1983). The survey team must realize, however, that the corners it is cutting to save time may need to be explained later to upper management.

Are Fatigue Effects an Issue?

Fatigue effects can occur when respondents become tired, bored, or sleepy as a result of questionnaire length. This problem is most likely to occur when respondents are asked to rate or respond to a long list of very similar items. Keeping the survey as short as possible, using self-administered surveys, or providing a break are ways of reducing fatigue effects caused by long surveys.

If the respondents are already tired or sleep deprived when they arrive to take the survey, it may not take much for them to exhibit fatigue effects. A colleague of ours who was administering surveys to new recruits in a military boot camp learned the meaning of fatigue effects quite dramatically. The recruits, who typically work hard all day and get only a few hours of sleep each night, often fell asleep at their desks while completing the survey. Part of our colleague's regular administration procedure was to walk around the room and gently awaken sleepy sailors. Although most survey teams will not have fatigue effects this dramatic, even small amounts of fatigue can result in respondents not concentrating fully on the survey.

What Is the Bottom Line on Survey Length?

The survey should be just long enough to allow all the issues it must cover to be covered. If possible, it is usually a good idea to include several items per topic on the survey. A group of items is generally a more reliable measure than a single item measuring the same issue. Some important topics that the survey is supposed to address might be split into several subtopics or facets—each of which would be scored separately.

The survey team should not, however, get carried away and write dozens of survey items per topic. Eventually, the survey would become so long that respondents would not complete it, even if permitted to do so on company time. Every item in an organizational survey should be included because it assesses a topic consistent with the goals of the survey. Survey items should not be included just because the responses might be interesting or the item is the favorite of a survey team member or someone in management. In general, we agree with Sheatsley (1983), who notes that "most questionnaires are too long, rather than too short, in that many of the items are found to contribute little or nothing to the analysis" (p. 223). Reaching a consensus on survey length involves the difficult task of narrowing down the item pool to only the most essential items.

Ordering the Items, or Putting It All Together

This section provides an overview of how to arrange the items on the survey instrument. The two aspects of arranging that we discuss are whether or not to group together all the items for a dimension and how to deal with possible item order effects.

Clustering Versus Scattering the Items for a Single Dimension

When all the survey items are written, the next step is to place them in order on the survey. Survey developers disagree on whether all the items from each dimension should be presented together or mixed with items from other dimensions. Some organizational survey instruments such as the Job Descriptive Index (a measure of job satisfaction; Smith, Kendall, & Hulin, 1969) have all the items for a given dimension listed together. Other instruments such as the Survey of Work Values (Wollack, Goodale, Wijting, & Smith, 1971) have items from the various dimensions interspersed throughout the survey. Some survey developers believe they can control biases better if the topic areas being measured are not obvious, whereas other survey experts contend that respondents give more accurate, well-thought-out answers when questions on the same topic are placed next to each other.

In general, our preference is to group related items together. If the survey seems illogical and scattered to respondents and is difficult for them to follow, some respondents may become annoyed or frustrated and may even fail to complete the survey. Furthermore, we generally try to order the survey questions within clusters of homogeneous items to make it easier for respondents to answer. For example, we might start with questions regarding specific characteristics about the job, followed by items regarding general characteristics of the job, followed by an overall assessment of the job. This ordering aids the respondents' recall and helps to ensure that respondents consider all the components before rendering their overall assessments. Filter questions, which ask respondents if a certain condition applies to them (e.g., "Do you have children?"), should be placed just prior to questions to which they are logically related (e.g., questions about child care issues).

Item Order Effects

The order in which items are presented in an organizational survey can affect the responses obtained (Oskamp, 1991). An *item order effect* occurs when an answer to a later item is influenced by previous items, response alternatives, or answers. For example, if respondents are asked a number of personal, sensitive questions at the beginning of a survey (e.g., whether or not they have abused drugs and alcohol, violated company rules, or are actively seeking employment elsewhere), their responses to later more innocuous questions may be colored by their reactions to the personal, sensitive items.

One way to reduce item order effects is through careful organization of the survey. Simple, nonthreatening, factual items should go first, and sensitive questions should appear later (Sheatsley, 1983). Similarly, the survey team may be concerned that some respondents will view answers to the demographic items (e.g., gender and race or ethnicity) as reducing their degree of confidentiality or anonymity, especially when the survey topics are intrusive or sensitive.

Alreck and Settle (1985) identify another type of item order effect—*initiation effect.* An initiation effect can occur if respondents are unsure how to answer an early set of items. Their responses may change as they become more familiar with the topic. Clear instructions and practice or example items before major sections can reduce the influence of initiation effects.

Some Practical Advice

The survey should be assembled so that it is as easy and painless as possible for respondents to read and complete. To the extent possible, smooth transitions should be included to span the different sections on the survey. Respondents become annoyed if every question on the survey seems to address a different, unrelated topic. If topics change suddenly, a brief explanation or transition between the sections can be added. These steps should go a long way toward preserving the respondents' goodwill.

Conclusions

This chapter and the previous one introduced survey teams to the art and practice of item writing. Although the number and content of the guidelines in these two chapters may seem overwhelming and bewildering at first glance, experience in writing items will result in many of these rules and regulations becoming routine and automatic. Survey team members who write items regularly will begin to develop a sixth sense for detecting bad items, identifying the best format to measure the characteristic of concern, minimizing the potential for response bias, and displaying the survey content in the best manner possible.

Note

1. Although *scale* is probably the most common way to refer to such a homogeneous group of items, we have elected to limit the use of this term to the rating formats (e.g., a 5-point scale). Confusion occurs when *scale* is used to refer to both (a) the rating continuum for answering each individual item and (b) the collection of several items that measure a similar characteristic.

Selecting Survey Respondents

5

This chapter is designed to help the reader determine who will be asked to complete the survey. The first step is to identify the population of interest. Once this task is completed, the team is better able to decide whether organizational survey information should be gathered from the population or from a sample (a subset of the population). Additional questions await the survey team that elects to use a sample. These questions fall into two broad areas: what type of sampling should be used and how large the sample should be.

Identifying the Target Population

The first step in determining who will receive an organizational survey is to define the *target population* (Kalton, 1983). The target population is the ideal group of all individuals who possess knowledge and views pertinent to the survey content. In many surveys, the target population will be all members of the organization. In other cases, the target population will be a subset of the organization's personnel. The target population for a climate survey might be everyone in the organization, whereas the target population for a survey of satisfaction with on-site child care would be only organizational members who have young children.

At times, using the target population may lead to practical problems. For example, an organization is planning to move its corporate headquarters to another city. An organization must assess employee relocation intentions and report the results within a few weeks. Because the organization is small, everyone in the organization will be surveyed. Some of the employees will, however, be on vacation or at training during the short survey period. Therefore, the survey team defines its population as organization members who are at work during the week of survey administration.

In this hypothetical case, constraints placed on the target population led to defining the population as members who actually received the survey—the *survey population* (Kalton, 1983). Kalton (1983) notes that "the advantage of starting with the ideal target population is that the exclusions are explicitly identified, thus enabling the magnitude and consequences of the restriction to be assessed" (p. 7). Because survey teams will most likely deal with constraints and exclusions in their population definition, future references (in this book) to the population are to the more restricted survey population.

Should the Population or a Sample Be Used in Data Collection?

On a practical level, conducting a census (i.e., sending a survey to everyone in the population) may be logistically and financially impossible. At the same time, sending a survey to all members of the population can lead to positive outcomes that are especially important considerations in organizational surveys. Sending the survey to everyone increases the "face validity" of the findings and suggests that management cares enough about employees to ask for their input. Surveying the population also provides all employees with a vehicle for communicating their true feelings to management.

When the population is large, conducting a census is seldom necessary from a statistical perspective. Responses drawn from a carefully selected, representative sample can allow for accurate generalizations to the population (Henry, 1990). As the famous pollster George Gallup noted, "an accurate blood test requires only a few drops of blood" (quoted in Kagay & Elder, 1992, p. E-5). The political polls that dominate U.S. news take advantage of this fact. Findings from surveys of 1,500 or fewer respondents often generalize to the entire U.S. population with a small margin of error due to sampling.

Our informal poll of organizational survey practices in the San Diego area found that about three quarters of the responding organizations typically give their surveys to all employees, whereas the remaining one quarter use sampling. We highly recommend that everyone be surveyed in organizations with 500 or fewer members. Given the fact that most organizations fall into this category, we present only a cursory overview of the basic sampling issues that a survey team might encounter when dealing with larger populations. If our overview and examples suggest that sampling should be considered further, the reader might want to refer to Henry's (1990) *Practical Sampling* or Rea and Parker's (1992) *Designing and Conducting Survey Research: A Comprehensive Guide*. Both books present in-depth and understandable coverage of survey sampling.

Assuming that a survey team decides that sampling is appropriate, consideration must be given to how the sample will be chosen. There are two basic types of samples: probability and nonprobability samples.

Probability Sampling

Probability sampling is needed if a survey team wishes to generalize sample-derived findings to the population. Probability sampling has several important characteristics (Rea & Parker, 1992). First, the probability of any member of the survey population being selected for inclusion in the sample is known. Second, all members of the survey population have an equal chance of being selected for the sample.[1] Third, the selection of one individual for the sample is independent of the selection of any other individual. The basic assumption in probability sampling is that the people who are selected for the sample are just like the people who are not selected (Fink & Kosecoff, 1985). Thus, the use of probability sampling requires an up-to-date list of all members of the survey population (i.e., a *sampling frame*).

Organizations typically use one of two probability sampling methods: simple random sampling or stratified sampling. Henry (1990) describes these and other more complex sampling procedures in detail.

Simple Random Sampling

Simple random sampling is the easiest, most straightforward sampling method (Henry, 1990). Everyone in the survey population has an equal chance of being selected for the sample. If this condition is met, the resulting sample should be representative of the larger population.

Before the widespread use of computers, a table of random numbers was used to select individuals from the survey frame. The probability sampling process is much simpler when information (e.g., name or organizational identification number) on all population members is available in a computerized database. Many statistical packages for computers contain simple routines that automatically generate a probability sample. For example, the SPSS-X (SPSS, 1988) sample command needs to know only the number of cases to be selected and the size of the population (or total subgroup). If a random sample of 1,200 members is to be drawn from a population of 15,036 people, the command is SAMPLE 1200 FROM 15036.

Stratified Sampling

In *stratified sampling,* the survey team assigns each individual from the population to a stratum, or subgroup, before conducting random sampling within each stratum. Each individual falls into only one subgroup, and everyone within that group stands an equal probability of being included in the sample. Stratified sampling is used when a survey team wants to ensure adequate representation of subgroups that have particular importance to the issues being surveyed (Henry, 1990). Because a stratified sample is more representative of the population from which it is drawn, it will result in more precise survey estimates.

Some of the more common stratification variables in organizational surveys are gender (female and male), race (e.g., white, black, Hispanic, Asian/Pacific Islander, Native American/Eskimo), organizational level (e.g., management, clerical), and department (e.g., production, marketing, sales). In more complex stratified sampling designs, it is necessary to cross the levels of two or more different stratification variables. For example, a survey team seeking opinions about proposed incentive plans might stratify the sample on both organizational level and department. In this case,

TABLE 5.1 Numbers and Percentages of Managers and Hourly Workers at
Organization Sites: The Population

Organization Site	Type of Employee		Total
	Managers	*Hourly Workers*	*Total*
Headquarters	40 (1%)	190 (4%)	230 (5%)
Plant A	240 (6%)	1,500 (35%)	1,750 (41%)
Plant B	300 (7%)	2,000 (47%)	2,300 (54%)
Total	580 (14%)	3,690 (86%)	4,270 (100%)

the survey team would divide individuals into all the subgroups of interest (e.g., production managers, sales clerks) and then select a random sample of each subgroup to receive the survey.

▨ *Proportionate Stratified Sampling*

In *proportionate stratified sampling,* the same percentage of people (e.g., 10%) is chosen from each subgroup. Therefore, the proportional representation of each subgroup is the same in both the sample and the population.

Table 5.1 shows that Organization X has 4,270 employees. It also shows the number of managers and hourly workers at headquarters and at Plants A and B. The numbers in parentheses indicate the approximate percentage of the population represented at each site and/or organizational level. For example, 190 (or 4%) of Organization X's 4,270 members are hourly employees who work at the headquarters.

After examining its budget, the Organization X survey team decided it could afford to survey around 430 employees (or about 10% of the population). Because the team wanted to generalize survey findings from the sample to the overall population, only proportionate stratified sampling was used. The survey team classified each person in the population as a manager or an hourly worker at one of the three organization locations. The team then randomly chose 10% ($n = 427$) of the organization members in each group to serve as the sample.

Table 5.2 shows the composition of the sample. Note that the percentage of each subgroup in the Table 5.2 sample equals the percentage of that subgroup in the Table 5.1 population.

Why use proportionate stratified sampling instead of a simple random sample? When using simple random sampling, the survey team hopes that random selection results in a sample that reflects the various subgroups in the population. The possibility exists, however, that the simple random sample will not be representative of all population strata. Proportionate stratified sampling guarantees appropriate representation of key popula-

TABLE 5.2 Numbers and Percentages of Managers and Hourly Workers at Organization Sites: A Proportionate Stratified Sample

Organization Site	Type of Employee		Total
	Managers	*Hourly Workers*	*Total*
Headquarters	4 (1%)	19 (4%)	23 (5%)
Plant A	24 (6%)	150 (35%)	174 (41%)
Plant B	30 (7%)	200 (47%)	230 (54%)
Total	58 (14%)	369 (86%)	427 (100%)

tion subgroups and, relative to simple random sampling, typically results in more precise survey estimates by reducing sampling error (Henry, 1990).

▨ *Disproportionate Stratified Sampling*

At other times, analysis of subgroup responses is a primary aim of the survey team. For example, most of the Organization X sample consists of hourly workers from Plants A and B. In fact, responses would be gathered from only four managers at headquarters (assuming they all responded to the survey). This illustration raises a key point that is brought up periodically throughout this book. We caution against reporting subgroup data when there are fewer than 10 people in a stratum. This caution has two bases. For groups of fewer than 10 people, anonymity can be compromised and findings are unstable since they are based on small numbers.

If subgroup analysis is planned (e.g., because there are rumors about dissatisfaction among headquarters managers and their input is especially desired), it is important to make sure that all subgroups are represented in reasonable numbers. In such cases, disproportionate sampling should be used. With this strategy, different sampling fractions are used for different sample strata. Therefore, all members of the population do not have an equal chance of selection (although there is an equal probability of selecting any given person within a stratum), and subgroup representation in the sample will not reflect that of the population.

Table 5.3 shows a disproportionate sampling strategy that increases the representation of smaller population subgroups but keeps the overall sample size (*n* = 425) approximately the same. Again, the number of sample members from each stratum is given, along with the percentage of the entire sample that each stratum represents. In addition, the sampling percentage within each stratum is shown in bold.

The percentages in bold in Table 5.3 show very different or disproportionate chances of being selected for participation in the survey. Because headquarters has relatively few managers, half the people in this condition

TABLE 5.3 Numbers and Percentages of Managers and Hourly Workers at Organization Sites: A Disproportionate Stratified Sample

| | Type of Employee | | |
Organization Site	*Managers*	*Hourly Workers*	*Total*
Headquarters	20 (5%)	80 (19%)	100 (24%)
	50%	**42%**	**43%**
Plant A	60 (14%)	90 (21%)	150 (35%)
	25%	**6%**	**9%**
Plant B	70 (16%)	105 (25%)	175 (41%)
	23%	**5%**	**8%**
Total	150 (35%)	275 (65%)	425 (100%)
	26%	**5%**	

were selected. This 50% selection ratio stands in stark contrast to the percentages of hourly workers who were selected from Plants A and B. In each case, less than 10% of the stratum was selected to receive the survey.

The drawback of disproportionate stratified sampling is that the subgroups in the sample and population are not reflected in the same proportions. For example, Plant B hourly workers constituted 47% of the total population of 4,270 employees but only 25% of the sample of 425 employees. This situation is not a problem if the survey team desires only to make generalizations to the subgroup from which the disproportionate stratified sample came. More specifically, the survey could make a statement such as "Twenty-five percent of the hourly workers in Plant B believe that their opportunities for advancement are good."

Additional steps are required to generalize findings from the disproportionate stratified sample to either the total organization population or to one of the five marginal or aggregate conditions: all managers, all hourly workers, all headquarters employees, or all Plant A or Plant B employees. The data need to be adjusted statistically to compensate for the disproportionate stratified sampling. Such adjustments are called *poststratification weighting* and are described in Chapter 10. Once the adjustments are made, the survey team can make statements such as "Forty percent of the people in this organization believe that their opportunities for advancement are good" or "Twenty-five percent of Organization X managers believe that their opportunities for advancement are good."

Nonprobability Sampling

Sometimes population information is not available, resources are short, or time pressures do not allow a survey team to choose a probability sample. In *nonprobability sampling,* the chance that a particular individual will be chosen as part of a sample is unknown. Therefore, the survey team cannot assume that all members of a population have an equal chance of being selected. Rather, subjective judgment plays a role in who is selected for the sample (Henry, 1990). Two examples illustrate how nonprobability samples might be used and the problems that can result.

Convenience Sample

A *convenience sample* is just that—participants are people who are convenient and available. For example, a survey team might use a convenience sample when conducting a survey of satisfaction with cafeteria services. The members could stand outside the company cafeteria and ask people who have just eaten to complete a questionnaire before returning to work.

Although convenience samples are easy to get, the obtained data may not answer the desired questions. If a primary goal of the cafeteria survey is to increase the number of people who eat there, questions must be asked about why personnel do not use the facility. With a convenience sample, data are being gathered only from people already eating at the cafeteria, rather than peers who might be enticed to eat there if changes were made (e.g., by lowering prices or offering more variety).

Quota Sampling

Quota sampling is another nonprobability sampling procedure. Like convenience sampling, it presents problems when there is a need to generalize findings to the population. For quota sampling, each team member might survey a fixed percentage, say, 10% of the people in a given department. The choice of whom to survey is left to the team members and department supervisors. As a result, all respondents may be friends of a team member and share the team member's perceptions about the issues of interest. Or the supervisor might have ulterior motives in deciding which subordinates complete the survey (e.g., it is easier to spare less productive workers or the supervisor sends the workers who are most likely to have favorable views).

In conclusion, these examples illustrate why generalizations to a population should not be made from a nonprobability sample. Such conclusions may be quite erroneous!

Sampling Error and Sample Size

For survey teams in small organizations, deciding on the number of people who will be asked to complete a survey is a moot issue because everyone will be asked. The decision is considerably more complex for a survey team in a large organization that decides to use sampling. There is no quick or easy prescription for identifying the ideal sample size. We provide the guidelines that we use. These rules of thumb should prove adequate for most situations.

Sampling Error

If everyone in a population is surveyed and most of the surveys are returned, the results should accurately reflect the views and behaviors of the population (assuming, of course, that measurement error, nonresponse error, and response bias are low). When a sample is used, the results may be close to the population values, but not exactly the same. *Sampling error* (also called *standard error* by Henry, 1990) is the degree to which a statistic from a sample can be expected to vary from the value that would have been obtained if the data were gathered from the population (Edwards & Thomas, 1993). Sampling error is influenced by two factors: how much variability exists in the issue or variable being measured and the size of the sample. If most people agree about a particular issue being surveyed, the data have little sampling error. Similarly, sampling error is low for a statistic derived from a large sample. In addition, power (the probability of detecting an effect if the effect really exists in the population) is increased as sample size gets larger.

Most people are familiar with the concept of sampling error as it is applied to political and opinion polls. For example, a newspaper article might report that in a representative nationwide sample, 54% of those surveyed believed that the president is doing a good job. This type of poll may also report a margin of error, often either ±3% or ±5%. Margin of error is another way of saying sampling error. If the margin of error for the prior example is ±5%, the population value very likely falls between 49% (54% – 5%) and 59% (54% + 5%).

Our statement has been qualified by saying that the population value "very likely" falls within the specified interval. The true value cannot be known with absolute certainty unless the entire population is measured. We can, however, stipulate a desired *degree of confidence* for the results. The most commonly used degrees of confidence are 95% and 99%. A degree of confidence of 95% (also called the *confidence interval*) means that we could expect that the true population values in the above example would be between 49% and 59% in 95 out of 100 instances. If we wish to be more certain that the population value is being correctly estimated (say, 99 times out of 100) for the same set of data, the interval around the sample statistics (54%) becomes considerably larger.

Sample Size

▦ *Minimum Sample Size*   The desired degrees of both sampling error and confidence must be considered when deciding on an appropriate sample size.[2] Numerous formulas exist to calculate required sample size. Table 5.4 uses one of these formulas to provide minimum sample sizes for selected populations.[3] These values are based on the assumption that a proportion (such as the percentages of personnel who respond "Yes" or "No" to a particular question) is the primary statistic of interest. Rea and Parker (1992) and Henry (1990) provide formulas for calculating sample sizes with larger populations and for interval-level data (e.g., Likert scales).

Sample sizes get larger with increased confidence intervals and decreased margin of error (sampling error). After a certain point, sample size does not increase in proportion to population size. The sample needed from a population of 100,000 at 95% confidence and with a 5% margin of error

TABLE 5.4 Minimum Sample Sizes for Selected Small Populations

Population Size (N)	95% Confidence			99% Confidence		
	±3%	±5%	±10%	±3%	±5%	±10%
200*	100a	100a	65	100a	100a	91
300	150a	150a	72	150a	150a	107
400	200a	200a	78	200a	200a	118
500	250a	218	81	250a	250a	125
750	325a	255	86	325a	325a	136
1,000	500a	278	88	500a	399	143
1,250	576	294	90	625a	434	146
1,500	624	306	91	750a	460	150
1,750	664	316	92	875a	482	152
2,000	696	323	92	959	499	154
2,250	724	329	93	1,013	513	155
2,500	748	334	93	1,061	525	156
3,000	788	341	94	1,142	544	158
3,500	818	347	94	1,207	558	159
4,000	843	351	94	1,262	569	160
4,500	863	354	94	1,308	578	160
5,000	880	357	95	1,347	586	161
7,500	935	366	95	1,479	610	163
10,000	965	370	96	1,556	622	164
15,000	997	375	96	1,641	635	164
20,000	1,014	377	96	1,687	642	165
50,000	1,045	382	96	1,777	655	166
75,000	1,053	383	96	1,798	658	166
100,000	1,056	383	96	1,809	659	166

NOTES: *If the population is less than 200, the entire group should be used.

a. Population sizes for which the assumption of normality does not apply. In such cases, the sample size should be 50% of the population size (Rea & Parker, 1992).

($n = 383$) is not that different from the sample size needed for a population of 10,000 ($n = 370$).

▨ *Actual Sample Size* The values in Table 5.4 are the minimum sample sizes you must achieve for the chosen margin of error and confidence level. In all likelihood, the actual sample size will need to be sufficiently larger than those indicated in Table 5.4 because of ineligibles (people in the target population who are not available to complete a survey) and nonrespondents (people who receive the survey but choose not to complete it). Henry (1990, p. 125) provides a formula that simultaneously corrects for ineligibles and non-response. This formula for the adjusted n (i.e., n') is

$$n' = \frac{n}{(e)(r)}$$

where *n* is the minimum sample size, *e* is the proportion of eligible respondents on the list, and *r* is the response rate expected.

As an example, Organization X has 4,270 people. The survey team wants a simple random sample of personnel. For a 5% margin of error and a 95% level of confidence, responses from about 354 people need to be gathered to make generalizations to the population. The survey team estimates that about 95% of the target population will be available to fill out the survey, and it expects a response rate of about 87%.

$$N' \text{ (the adjusted } n) = \frac{354}{(.95)(.87)} = 428.$$

Therefore, 428 surveys should be administered to obtain the necessary minimum sample size.

Remember that the Table 5.4 entries are minimum sample sizes. Make sure the budget covers the actual sample size needed to obtain the desired number of returned surveys.

▦ *Sample Size and Subgroups*

Rea and Parker (1992) suggest that, as a rule of thumb, a 10% margin of error is the maximum error that should be tolerated for any sample stratum or substratum. To achieve a 10% margin of error, data from at least 100 people must be gathered. At times, 100 people may not exist in a particular subgroup. Care should be used when interpreting data from small strata; the margin of error can be very large.

▦ *A Final Note on Sample Size*

Table 5.4 shows that between about 100 and 1,800 people can serve as minimum samples to survey a population of 100,000 people. The survey team must remember, however, that a minimum sample may not be a credible sample. Statistically unsophisticated organization members may not believe that a sample of 400 people can adequately represent an organization of 15,000 employees. As a result, questions about the validity of the findings and conclusions may be raised (Weisberg & Bowen, 1977). This outcome is especially likely when managers or employers do not like the survey results. Decisions about sample size should be made primarily on the basis of the data analysis plan, that is, the number of subgroups for whom results will later be presented. The survey team should also take into consideration the nature of the organization, the audience to whom the results will be presented, and the audience's understanding of sampling procedures when deciding on sample size.

Although justified on statistical grounds, sampling may conflict with the previously cited communication function of organizational surveys. If only a portion of the organization receives the survey, the ability of all employees to communicate with management decreases. Lower employee involvement in the survey process may impede the success of change efforts that follow from survey results (Paul & Bracken, 1995).

Sampling may increase organizational rivalries and mistrust. Individuals chosen for the sample may wonder why they were selected and whether they are being singled out in a negative way. Individuals not chosen may feel left out or deprived of the opportunity to voice their views. Thus, although administering a survey to more people than is statistically necessary may be wasteful in terms of financial costs, time delays, and expenditure of resources, there may be times when the more-is-merrier approach is justified by other considerations.

Notes

1. With a probability sample, some segments of the population can be selected at higher probabilities than others, as long as the probability is known.

2. Henry (1990) terms this decision *tolerable error*—standard (sampling) error multiplied by the z value that represents the confidence level of choice.

3. The values in Table 5.4 were calculated using Rea and Parker's (1992) formula for small samples (containing a finite population correction) and questions involving proportions. The formula is:

$$\frac{Z_\alpha^2(.25)N}{Z_\alpha^2(.25)+(N-1)C_p^2}$$

where EMBED Equation.2 is the z score that represents the desired confidence interval (1.96 for 95% confidence and 2.575 for 99% confidence), N is the population size, and EMBED Equation.2 is the desired margin of error (.03, .05, .10).

Organizational Survey Administration

6

Now that the team has decided on the content of the survey and the characteristics of the people who will be asked to respond, it is time to determine the mechanics of how the survey data will be gathered. These mechanics are collectively known as *survey administration procedures.* Administration procedures include the settings (e.g., alone vs. in groups) in which people receive the survey instrument, the format or mode through which they are presented the survey (e.g., paper vs. computer vs. interview), and the method of return (e.g., mail vs. drop box).

A primary issue is whether a self- or group-administered survey is more advantageous. Answers to this concern must be considered together with sample size, survey content, and other factors to select the appropriate administration technique. We review four major survey administration techniques: paper, computer, face-to-face interview, and telephone interview.

Self- Versus Group-Administered Surveys

An important decision in the organizational survey process is whether the survey should be self- or group-administered. In a *self-administered survey,* a respondent receives a packet individually in the mail (Postal Service or interoffice) or is given the survey at work, usually by a member of the survey team. Self-administered surveys typically provide a high degree of anonymity and confidentiality and are often the method of choice for surveys containing sensitive items. Self-administration is also a good way to survey highly specialized groups (Sheatsley, 1983) such as recent car buyers or members of professional organizations. A self-administered survey has an advantage with regard to when it will be completed: Respondents are allowed to choose when it is most convenient to fill out the questionnaire. Similarly, self-administered surveys are usually preferred when the potential respondents to an organizational survey are not employees of the organization (e.g., college alumni).

In a *group-administered survey,* the respondents are gathered in a group setting, typically at their work site, and given the survey by a survey administrator who is present to answer any questions. Group-administered surveys produce very high response rates. In our experience, very few people decline to complete a survey once they have been assembled with other respondents. Also, group administration allows the survey team to control the conditions under which the data are collected. Much greater standardization and uniformity can be achieved because one person can collect data from a large number of individuals and groups. For example, a survey administrator can minimize the amount of discussion that respondents have while completing the survey. The survey administrator has a chance to explain the purpose of the survey, and respondents are able to ask questions. Administering surveys in groups typically results in a relatively short data-gathering period. A survey team might be able to gather the data in a week or less using group administration in an organization with only one or two sites.

There are disadvantages to both approaches. With self-administered surveys, the team is not sure that the person who received the survey is the one who completed it or that the intended respondent did not ask someone for assistance (Sheatsley, 1983). Self-administered surveys—especially individual mail-outs—are labor intensive to distribute, as well as costly and slow. It may take several months to get the surveys back, more if repeated follow-up procedures are used. Another disadvantage of self-administered surveys is that they usually do not provide respondents an opportunity to get clarification on questions or sections of the survey that they do not understand.

There are several disadvantages to group-administered surveys. Although one part of the organization (e.g., the human resource department) may be very enthusiastic about the survey, other departments may be cynical or distrusting. Consequently, some supervisors may object to allowing their subordinates to come to the group administration site. Thus, to ensure that supervisors grant release time from work so that respondents can show up for group administration, the team needs to communicate to supervisors the importance of the effort and try to enlist supervisors as allies of the survey process rather than potential adversaries.

In a group-administered survey situation, it may be difficult to convince respondents that their answers are truly anonymous or confidential. Some of our respondents have suggested that their handwriting could be used to identify them or that they could be found out by an analysis of the survey demographics. In such cases, answers to a group-administered survey might suffer from social desirability responding. As Bourque and Clark (1992) note, "when questionnaires are administered to groups of respondents, the respondents' perceptions of the researcher or the location may cause them to change their answers to fit their perceptions of the responses desired" (p. 3).

TABLE 6.1   A Comparison of Self- and Group-Administered Surveys

	Self-Administered Surveys	*Group-Administered Surveys*
Which administration methods can be used?	Paper, scanner, fax, individual computer, networked computer	Paper, scanner, networked computer
When will the survey be completed?	At a time chosen by the respondent	At time(s) chosen by the survey administrator
Where is the survey completed?	In a setting chosen by the respondent	In setting(s) chosen by the survey administrator
Who oversees the survey administration?	The respondent	The survey administrator
How much control is there of the conditions under which data are gathered?	Less control	More control
Which administration method results in more completed surveys?	Lower percentage completed	Higher percentage completed
How much time is required for the data-gathering period?	Usually longer	Usually shorter
What is the relative cost of the two survey-administration methods?	Dependent on several factors but usually has greater direct costs such as printing and mailing	Dependent on several factors but usually has greater indirect costs such as personnel time
How much anonymity and confidentiality can be given respondents?	High anonymity, high confidentiality	Although responses may be anonymous, participation is not; confidentiality of responses can still be maintained

In addition to reduced feelings of anonymity, guarantees of confidentiality may be less effective in group-administered surveys. Even though respondents are told that their responses are confidential (i.e., not shown to others), their participation in the survey may in fact be generally known. Thus, at some later point they may fear being associated with or blamed by others for the survey results. For example, if a supervisor is given survey feedback that her subordinates view her as having poor leadership skills, the supervisor may associate the poor ratings with the individuals in her work group who were chosen to participate in the survey. Despite these misgivings, respondents in group-administered surveys may not feel comfortable refusing to fill out a survey in the presence of coworkers or supervisors, thus adding an element of implicit coercion. Finally, although survey teams on a tight budget may choose group distribution simply to keep direct costs (e.g., postage, paper, envelopes) down, the indirect costs (e.g., time respondents use to go to and from a central survey site) may make group administration as costly or even more expensive than self-administration. Table 6.1 provides a comparison of self- and group-administered surveys.

Modes of Survey Administration

Selecting the most appropriate survey administration mode—whether paper, computer, e-mail, face-to-face interview, or telephone—depends on factors such as the number of respondents desired, how fast the information must be collected, the depth of information needed, and the degree of anonymity required (Booth-Kewley, Rosenfeld, & Edwards, 1993). Each mode has advantages and disadvantages. This section discusses those strengths and weaknesses and describes the general procedures for each administration mode. We begin with the most commonly used mode—paper surveys.

Paper Surveys

There are three major types of paper (also called *paper-and-pencil*) surveys: traditional paper, generic scannable, and customized scannable.

▨ Traditional Paper

The traditional paper survey is still by far the most common type of survey. For example, restaurants, hotels, and other organizations often have comment cards containing short surveys requesting feedback about their services. Similarly, surveys asking for demographic and other types of data are routinely included with the warranty cards for products consumers purchase.

Because of its longer history and more frequent use, the traditional paper survey is the standard against which other survey administration modes are compared. Our informal survey of organizational survey practices in the San Diego area found that a large majority of the responding organizations administered their surveys using the traditional paper method. One reason traditional paper continues to be the most popular survey administration mode is because it is the easiest to compose. The survey is printed on paper, and the respondent answers the items on the survey booklet by completing scales, choosing among several alternatives, or writing narrative answers to open-ended questions.

Traditional paper surveys have a number of other important strengths: ease and efficiency of administration, inexpensiveness to duplicate, and familiarity to those being surveyed. Furthermore, paper surveys are less likely than in-person interviews to elicit socially desirable responding (Martin & Nagao, 1989). Their administration does not require interview skills, technical expertise, or sophisticated equipment.

Traditional paper surveys also have a number of drawbacks. Manually entering responses from paper surveys into a computer for data analysis is time consuming and can lead to errors. Respondents completing paper surveys may leave out answers to some items, resulting in missing data. As we shall show in Chapter 9, missing data may make it difficult or impossible to determine respondents' scores on multiple-item dimensions (e.g., job satisfaction). Respondents using paper surveys may answer inappropriately, such as by giving multiple responses to a single question when only one response is requested. In other cases, a survey team may want respondents to omit a subset of items depending on how a prior item is answered. This omission procedure is known as item branching or a skip pattern. If respondents become confused with the instructions, too many or too few items may be skipped. Other administration modes minimize these problems.

▩ *Scannable Surveys: Generic and Customized*

On *scannable surveys,* respondents indicate their answers by filling in circles, ovals, or squares on a special form or by printing a letter or number in one or more blocks. A scanner reads the responses using one of two methods. *Transoptic scanning* sends light through the survey form and reads the intensity of the light on the other side of the form. *Reflective scanning* bounces light off one side of the form and measures the intensity of the reflected light (Booth-Kewley et al., 1993). The scanned answers are automatically placed in a computer database.

Scannable surveys can be either generic or customized. A *generic scannable survey* presents the survey items on printed pages; separate answer sheets with bubbles are used for recording answers. Although generic scannable forms are less costly and time consuming to develop than customized scannable surveys, generic forms have some limitations. One disadvantage is that generic scannable sheets typically limit the number of alternatives that can be used for a single item. This restriction causes problems if the items require a scale that has more alternatives than the generic scannable form allows. For example, if the generic form allows only five alternatives per question but the questions from a previously developed organizational culture scale require seven alternatives, it would be impossible to administer the items as intended. In addition, generic forms are more cumbersome. Respondents must read the questions on one page and then record their responses on another. Interestingly, aptitude test research (Veit & Scruggs, 1986; Wise, Plake, Eastman, & Novak, 1987) has shown that few test takers record answers in the wrong bubbles when using generic scannable sheets.

On *customized scannable surveys,* the questions and response options are printed together, directly on the same page. This format looks more professional, is much less cumbersome for the respondent, and minimizes any errors that might occur when answers are recorded on a separate sheet. The downside of customized scannable surveys is that they take extra time and effort to design and are more expensive than traditional paper because customized forms require specialized printing and scanning equipment.

The cost of these necessary services and equipment must be considered before deciding to use scannable surveys. For some organizations, the benefits of owning the specialized equipment may be worth the costs. Such organizations include consulting firms specializing in conducting surveys and big organizations that routinely conduct large-scale surveys. For other organizations that want customized scannable surveys but do not want to purchase the equipment, it may be more economical to buy form design and scanning services from firms specializing in that type of work. The costs of these services are partially offset by the reduction of the time and expense involved in data entry, the decreased number of data entry errors, and the intangible benefits of a more professional-looking survey.

As the costs of scanner equipment and software continue to decrease, scannable surveys will become even more commonplace. Currently, at least one program (Remark OCR) uses a regular flatbed scanner to scan specially prepared forms. This is particularly useful for small sample surveys that use short questionnaires.

The ability of scannable surveys to eliminate manual data entry is an advantage that may partially explain their increased popularity for administering large-scale organizational surveys. Customized scannable forms have been used in large U.S. federal government personnel surveys to gather data on sexual harassment (Merit Systems Protection Board, 1988), employee turnover (Merit Systems Protection Board, 1989), and employees' perceptions of pay and working conditions (Merit Systems Protection Board, 1990).

▧ *Faxed Paper Surveys*

Faxing surveys to potential respondents adds a new twist to the delivery of paper questionnaires. Until recently, the procedure was limited to sending a faxed copy of the survey to and from the respondent and then manually entering the answers into the database. New software has automated the data entry step. Now, the survey team can create a customized scannable survey. The team faxes a survey to each respondent. When the respondent has completed and returned the survey, the fax modem of the answering computer reads the answers and stores the data in a computer file. Box 6.1 describes findings from two surveys that used faxed surveys.

The newness of the customized scannable fax survey makes it difficult to evaluate the potential of this method of paper survey delivery. Although there is little research, we suspect that its niche may be limited to short surveys (e.g., fewer than 5 pages) sent to relatively few respondents (e.g., fewer than 250 participants) who are located in widely dispersed offices. Problems such as getting a busy signal when trying to return the faxed survey may limit the sample size and the length of the survey. As we shall show below, e-mail surveys may be more practical than faxes for many modern office environments, although that may change as fax technology continues to become more sophisticated and widespread.

Computer-Administered Surveys

Until recently, the use of computers for administering surveys required specialized programming skills and hard-to-get or expensive equipment. With the increasing availability of computers has come widely available, lower-cost software that facilitates the administration of surveys via computer (Dunnington, 1993; Kuhnert & McCauley, 1996).

The availability of relatively inexpensive and increasingly sophisticated PCs has made computer administration of organizational surveys more popular (Booth-Kewley et al., 1993). A more recent development—

BOX 6.1.

Fax Surveys

As fax machines become nearly universal in the business world, faxes will probably be used more often as a survey administration method. Fax surveys have an advantage over mail-out surveys in that faxes can get to the respondent more quickly and can be sent back to the survey team faster. Some initial studies have confirmed that fax surveys are returned more quickly than mail-out surveys.

Dickson and MacLachlan (1992) sent either a mail-out or fax survey to a sample of 450 business schools. Although the survey results did not differ between the two administration modes, the fax surveys were returned faster.

Similar findings were reported by Vazzana and Bachmann (1994). They compared mail-out and fax surveys using an organization's customer database. Once again, the survey results were similar across administration modes. Although the response rates for mail-back (19.1%) and fax (20.8%) surveys did not significantly differ, the fax surveys were returned more quickly. More than one quarter of the returned surveys were faxed back within one day.

If time is of the essence, fax may be a good way to obtain survey responses quickly.

computer networks—has presented even greater opportunities for administering surveys on computers.

■ *Personal Computer-Based Surveys*

Computer surveys may be administered through software either preloaded on PCs devoted specifically to the survey or via diskettes mailed to respondents. If the survey and administration software are preloaded on a PC designated for that purpose, respondents need only to sit at the computer and begin the program. The instructions explain how to respond to the survey items, which keys to use (e.g., T for True and F for False), and how to change responses. Depending on the survey software, the respondent may or may not be allowed to skip items, change responses, or review previous items and answers.

Respondents do not need knowledge of computers or prior computer experience to complete computer-administered surveys. Moreover, all the instructions for completing a survey can be contained on two or three computer screens. We and our colleagues have administered computer surveys to employees at all organizational levels: supervisors, blue-collar employees, and even recruits going through military boot camp. Few respondents have needed personal assistance. In fact, most were able to answer the survey merely by following the instructions that appeared on the computer screen.

In a computer-administered survey, the respondent is typically given at least one practice item before the real survey questions are administered. Once the survey starts, the software presents only one item (and its alternatives or a rating scale if applicable) per screen. Each time the respondent answers a question, the next question is automatically displayed on the screen. If the respondent chooses an out-of-range response (e.g., a 6 for a scale that goes from 1 to 5), the computer stays on the same item (and perhaps beeps) until an acceptable response is made. If the question is open ended (e.g., number of round-trip miles to work), the respondent types in the answer. Once the final question is answered, the computer informs the respondent that the session is over and creates a data record containing the information that the respondent entered. Some current survey systems such as Ci3 (Sawtooth Software, 1994) have the additional capability to analyze the survey data after they have been gathered.

Computer administration can also be accomplished through what Dunnington (1993, p. 111) calls "questionnaire on a diskette." In this variation, the respondent receives a diskette containing both the survey and the administration software. Instead of calling up the questionnaire from an existing computer system, the respondent inserts the diskette into his or her PC or workstation disk drive and then accesses the survey by following instructions accompanying the diskette. Responses are saved on the diskette, which is returned to the survey team after the data have been collected. Depending on the nature of the survey and the organization being surveyed, many respondents can complete the survey on a single diskette, or each respondent can receive his or her own survey diskette.

If the questionnaire on a diskette approach is used, the survey team should perform a quality check after diskette copies of the questionnaire are made and before the disks are distributed. We are aware of an instance where as many as one third of the mailed survey diskettes proved to be defective. Also, it is a good idea to provide a phone number and contact person should respondents be unable to load the software or have problems completing the survey. When the completed diskettes are returned, they should first be checked for computer viruses. One large survey (Mitchell et al., 1995) that used this methodology found that about 1% of the returned diskettes contained viruses.

One reason computers have become an increasingly popular means of administering organizational surveys is that they provide many capabilities that can enhance the quality of survey data. One of the most important features of a computer-administered survey is its ability to branch between items in a way that is invisible to respondents. This custom tailoring of surveys provides the user with much flexibility in asking questions. Branching that would have taken many pages and involved complicated instructions on paper surveys is accomplished on the computer without respondents being aware that they are answering items that other respondents do not see. Computer technology also allows respondents to be presented with graphs and other visual information. This advantage would be useful if an organization were surveying its employees about things such as new uniforms or corporate logos.

A number of studies (e.g., Booth-Kewley et al., 1992; Erdman, Klein, & Greist, 1983) have shown that respondents find the computer format more enjoyable than paper surveys containing identical questions. Some authors (Booth-Kewley et al., 1992; Matheson & Zanna, 1988) suggest that responding on the computer may lead to higher levels of self-awareness. Other studies (Lukin, Dowd, Plake, & Kraft, 1985; Rozensky, Honor, Rasinski, Tovian, & Herz, 1986; Skinner & Allen, 1983) have found that respondents perceive computer administration as "faster." That is, time seemed to pass more quickly for computer respondents than for peers who responded on a paper survey. Research has also indicated that respondents perceive computerized assessment as more useful (Davis & Cowles, 1989) and regard the experience as more relevant (Rozensky et al., 1986).

▩ *Surveys on Networked Computer Systems*

With increasing numbers of organizations being connected to the Internet and the World Wide Web system or having their office computers linked to local area networks (LANs), some organizations are using the file sharing and e-mail capabilities of these systems to gather survey data. For example, to administer a survey using an organization's e-mail system, a survey team member might type the items as an e-mail message and electronically send the survey to potential respondents connected to the system. Respondents type their answers in the space before or after each item and then send the e-mail containing the answers and items back to a site or address designated by the organization. As in paper surveys, guarantees that the responses will be confidential and reminder notices to those who haven't completed the survey are appropriate. Interestingly, one of our colleagues was recently surveyed using networked computers both within her own organization (using a LAN) and across organizations (using the Internet) during the same 1-week period.

Parker (1992) describes using e-mail to survey AT&T employees about issues related to workers in foreign countries. Parker's survey team chose e-mail because the potential respondents were located all over the world. Also, they felt that potential respondents already received too many paper surveys and would be more likely to respond to a computer-administered survey. E-mail also has the advantages of being faster than company mail, less time consuming than telephone interviewing, and it can be delivered to the respondent directly. In contrast, a fax survey typically goes to the respondent's office. Parker found that response rates were higher for those who received the e-mail survey (68%) than for those who received the same survey in company mail (38%). It remains to be seen, however, whether the higher response rates of e-mail surveys will decrease as the novelty of e-mail decreases and the amount of junk e-mail increases.

▦ *Comparison of Computer- and Paper-Administered Surveys*

Compared to traditional paper administration, a number of advantages are associated with computer administration of organizational surveys. For example, when surveys are administered via computer, data entry takes place as the respondent completes the survey. This saves time and leads to more accurate data because one of the stages at which errors may be introduced into a database is skipped. Another advantage is that, in general, survey data collected on a computer will not contain out-of-range or missing responses. Whereas respondents can give values too high or too low or omit answers on a paper survey, they can be prevented from doing so on a computer-administered survey. In addition, with computer administration, complex item branching can be used to present respondents with the items that are relevant only to them.

There are also several disadvantages. Computers are less portable than paper surveys. They may not be as accessible for some jobs or at remote work sites. Also, computers are subject to equipment failure and software problems (e.g., the operating system on some computers may not support diskettes mailed to potential respondents). In addition, the survey team must consider the possible expense of purchasing specialized hardware and software. Finally, some people may feel intimidated by computers or think that "big brother" is monitoring their computer responses (Rosenfeld, Booth-Kewley, Edwards & Thomas, 1996).

In practical terms, the survey team needs to consider a number of factors before it decides to administer a computer survey. We recommend computer administration of an organizational survey if most of the following conditions are met:

▦ Ample computers (either stand-alone or networked) and software are available or rental funds exist.

▦ The survey is to be administered on a regular basis.

▦ Survey data are primarily closed-ended rather than narrative.

▦ Quick results are needed.

▦ Respondents can be gathered in a single or limited number of locations.

▦ Item branching is used.

▦ The number of respondents to be surveyed is 500 or less.

Face-to-Face Interview Surveys

Interviews are a popular means of survey administration. They are often the method of choice for sociologists and market survey researchers. Typically, the interviewer reads the instructions, questions, and alternatives and then records the respondents' answers. The face-to-face interaction allows the interviewer to probe or follow up unanticipated responses, note nonverbal reactions, and clarify the meaning of items the respondent may not understand. The quality of face-to-face interview data may be further enhanced by combining this technique with the capabilities of item branching from computer-administered surveys.[1]

Good interview surveys require that interviewers be well trained. Among the topics that should be covered in training are how nonverbal and verbal interviewer cues, such as nodding the head or agreeing with the interviewee, may lead to biased results. For this reason, the training might include critiquing and possibly videotaping future interviewers as they administer the survey to one another. Also, an effort should be made to ensure that all interviewers are coding answers the same way (i.e., there is interrater agreement). This step may require listening to several tapes, recording the answers, and checking the agreement among coders.

■ *Comparison of Face-to-Face Interview and Other Methods*

Organizational researchers and practitioners use interviews to gather survey data less frequently than social scientists and market researchers. This limited use of the face-to-face interview survey method is the result of a number of factors. Administration of an interview survey takes longer than paper- or computer-administered surveys. Survey interviewing is also more expensive, especially when training, travel, supervising, and paying interviewers are considered (Bourque & Clark, 1992). It is easier to survey large numbers of people using paper or computers than it is to administer interview surveys, which require an interviewer be present for each and every respondent. As a consequence, interview surveys often result in generalizations based on data from fewer respondents. Also, if interviewers are not trained or are poorly trained, the quality of data may be poor. Finally, because the interviewer represents a status figure and it is impossible for respondents in face-to-face interviews to feel completely anonymous, individuals may give more socially desirable responses in face-to-face interviews than with paper- or computer-administered surveys (Martin & Nagao, 1989).

Despite these negatives, face-to-face interview surveys have advantages over other methods. An interviewer has greater control over the survey process than with paper or computer surveys. Interview methodology allows the investigator to probe for a richer, more complete understanding of the responses. Thus, an interviewer has an opportunity to clarify respondents' answers that would not be followed up on paper or computer surveys. Also, some research indicates that face-to-face interviews give better-quality data because of the rapport that can be built up between the interviewer and the respondent (Fowler & Mangione, 1990). Lastly, more than the other methods, interview questions can be tailored, adapted, changed, or deleted based on a respondent's answers to previous questions.

Telephone Interview Surveys

Telephones are frequently used to conduct surveys or interviews with the general population. It seems that at least once every several weeks, we are called and asked to participate in a *telephone interview survey*. In practice, telephone interview surveys have been used mostly by social scientists, market researchers, and political pollsters, and less often to conduct employee surveys (Booth-Kewley et al., 1993).

▤ *Computer-Assisted*
Telephone Interviewing
Surveys

As telephone surveys have grown more complex, they have become increasingly susceptible to interviewer error, especially when filtering or branching questions are asked. This problem has led to attempts to automate the telephone survey process through the development of computer-assisted telephone interviewing (CATI) systems. In a CATI system, the telephone interview is controlled by a computer. The computer presents questions to the interviewer in the correct order, branches to other questions if required, issues error messages when responses are out of range, and stores responses in a database for subsequent analysis. U.S. government agencies such as the Census Bureau and the Department of Agriculture have used CATI systems for telephone surveys (Frey, 1989). By automating much of the survey process, CATI offers the gains in efficiency and error reduction provided by computer surveys. CATI systems also facilitate precise sampling while minimizing interviewer error in survey administration.

The typical CATI survey lasts 8 to 10 minutes (Dunnington, 1993), but some academic and federal CATI surveys require much longer. CATI surveys are usually performed by consulting firms specializing in such services because the installation and upkeep (e.g., caller salaries) of a fully networked CATI system is very expensive (Booth-Kewley et al., 1993; Dunnington, 1993). If the survey instrument is lengthy, and the sample is relatively large, the high cost of CATI will probably discourage its use. Ross (1992) notes that the typical U.S. Air Force paper survey costs about $2 per person, whereas an equivalent CATI survey costs between $33 and $60 per person, depending on survey length and complexity. It should be noted, however, that recent increases in postage as well as a greater tendency to send follow-up postcards and surveys to nonrespondents has increased costs of typical mail-out surveys well beyond Ross's $2 per person figure.

▤ *Other Telephone Survey*
Methods

Two other telephone interview survey methods have recently gained in popularity. One method has respondents push the buttons on their telephone to indicate answers to prerecorded questions. The fast turnaround time of this method allowed CBS News to broadcast the results of a national opinion poll within 24 hours after President Clinton gave his 1995 State of the Union speech. This procedure also has the advantage of saving money by eliminating the costs of interviewers.

The other telephone method has people (e.g., television viewers) call into numbers to register their opinions or vote about a given topic. Care needs to be used in generalizing the results from the nonscientific samples that respond to call-in telephone surveys. At this time, we are unaware of any organizational applications of this method.

▩ *Advantages and Disadvantages of Telephone Surveys*

Telephone surveys have a number of advantages over other methods. Compared with a mail-out paper survey, a very brief telephone survey may be less expensive than printing and delivering paper surveys or administering surveys on computer diskettes, especially when the costs involved in follow-up procedures are considered. Similarly, telephone-administered surveys are more efficient and much less expensive than face-to-face interview surveys (Fowler, 1988). In other cases, telephones may be the only way to gather interview data because people are becoming more hesitant about letting strangers into their homes for in-person interviews. Although this may not be relevant for potential respondents who are members of an organization and can be contacted during work, this issue is important for surveys (e.g., customer satisfaction surveys) that require inputs from nonmembers.

There are also disadvantages to telephone-administered organizational surveys. When an organizational survey is administered by telephone, employees may doubt the confidentiality and anonymity of their responses. Most organizations do not conduct surveys of their employees at their homes because there is concern about employees' rights to privacy. Telephone surveys are usually more expensive than surveys administered in group settings or through the organization's interoffice mail. Compared with face-to-face interviews, rapport is more difficult to establish in a telephone survey. Thus, it is not surprising that individuals are less likely to answer sensitive questions in a telephone interview than they are in person (Groves & Kahn, 1979). Additionally, the nature of a telephone interaction (e.g., people are often in a hurry) limits the type and number of questions and the use of visual materials. Finally, as answering machines become more prevalent, it may be harder to contact individuals who regularly screen their calls (Tuckel & Feinberg, 1991).

Conclusions

When choosing an administration method, a number of factors should be considered, including how quickly the survey information is needed, the type of data to be gathered (e.g., quantitative vs. qualitative), the resources (e.g., computers, scanners, telephone lines) that are available, whether the survey will assess sensitive topics, the number of respondents to be surveyed, and whether team members possess the needed specialized skills. The paper survey will probably be chosen in the vast majority of cases. It is usually the most convenient way to gather a great amount of information from a large number of people. If computer equipment is widely available, the survey team may want to administer the survey via computer to save data entry time and avoid errors and to give respondents a more enjoyable survey experience. If in-depth, narrative information is needed from a limited number of respondents and skilled interviewers are available, the organization may choose to use telephone or in-person survey interviews. There is no one ideal method of survey administration. Rather, the method that best gets the job done is the one that should be chosen.

Note

1. Saris's (1991) book, *Computer-Assisted Interviewing,* discusses how face-to-face interviews can be complemented by the branching capability that is possible with computer surveys. In addition to discussing the advantages and disadvantages of computer-assisted personal interviewing, Saris leads readers through the steps they need to perform to use this technique.

Fielding the Survey

7

Many nuts-and-bolts steps must still be accomplished before the survey is actually administered. For example, input may be needed from other personnel within the organization, and final approval may be required from top management. Depending on the mode of survey administration, it will be necessary to alert appropriate personnel about duplicating, mailing, and other requirements. Without sufficient prearrangements, the survey process can come to a grinding halt. And no one ever wants to explain to higher-level organization members why the survey is not going to go out on time!

Issues related to fielding the survey are reviewed in this chapter. The first step is to finish the survey instrument by adding an introduction and instructions. Then the survey needs to be pretested.[1] Information gathered through the pretesting process will be used to modify the survey and create the final instrument. At that point, the survey team should obtain final approval for the instrument and data-gathering process. As soon as the approval process is completed, the team can prepare and distribute the survey packets.

Adding the Finishing Touches to the Survey Instrument

Previous chapters discussed the development of survey content and the art of item writing. Although the items are the most important part of the instrument, serious consideration must be given to the initial sections of the survey: the introduction and the instructions. When written well, these sections can help convince a reluctant respondent to complete a survey he or she might have otherwise discarded.

Survey Introduction

An introduction should appear before respondents are instructed on how to complete the survey. In most situations, the introduction is provided on the initial or second page of the survey. In other cases, a cover letter may be used to supplement or replace the introductory survey information.

The introduction should ask respondents for their participation, mention the content or subject matter of the survey, explain why the survey is being conducted, indicate who is sponsoring the survey, and explain how the results of the survey will be used. The introduction should also state whether participation in the survey is voluntary, any consequences of failing to complete the survey, and whether responses are anonymous and will be held in confidence.

If a sample, rather than a census, is used, the introduction needs to tell respondents why they were selected. For example, we usually explain to those chosen for our survey samples that they were randomly picked by a computer program. This concern is especially appropriate if only a very specific subgroup of a population, such as female blue-collar employees, is asked to supply data. Near the end of the introduction, the team should include survey return instructions (e.g., "Please mail your completed survey back in the postage-paid preaddressed envelope at your earliest convenience"). The introduction should end by thanking respondents for their assistance and telling them that their input is appreciated.

Some or all of the introductory content can be incorporated into a cover letter. This letter might be a separate sheet or printed as one of the first pages of the survey booklet. A letter signed by a high-ranking official such as the organization's president or CEO is a good way to impart the survey's importance to potential respondents. It is also a way to obtain the commitment of someone high in the organization structure.[2] Depending on the survey topic and nature of the organization (e.g., composed primarily of blue-collar, unionized workers), the survey team may also want to include a supporting letter signed by the head of the union. Figure 7.1 provides an example of a cover letter that includes important introductory material.

Whether a cover letter or a straight introduction is used, concerns that respondents might have about completing the survey need to be addressed. The following are topics that, if appropriate to a particular survey, should be mentioned.

▨ *Distrust of Anonymity or Confidentiality Guarantees*

Even if the survey is anonymous, respondents may be afraid they will be connected to their specific answers. This concern is especially a problem if the survey contains detailed demographic questions or questions about very sensitive issues. In such cases, the following sentences may be helpful: "The information you provide will be grouped with the responses of others and will not be associated with any single individual. No one will see how you answered the survey except for the people who analyze the results."

If the survey requires identification, respondents may be afraid that their responses will be disclosed to others and hurt their position or reputation in the organization. Respondents should be told why identifying information is required (e.g., to link to other databases, to allow for follow-up surveys) and what steps will be taken to ensure that they will suffer no

March 3, 1996

Dear Participant:

Organization X is preparing to institute a new promotion system, which I hope will reflect the philosophies and beliefs of our employees. To accomplish this goal, we need to know how you feel about the current promotion system. We also want your suggestions for making the system better.

Please carefully and honestly answer each question. Be assured that all your responses will be anonymous and will be reported only in group form. Your individual responses will never be identified. Participation in the survey is completely voluntary. You may choose not to participate. If you decide not to complete the survey, your status in this organization will not be affected in any way.

Please mail your survey back in the postage-paid preaddressed envelope by March 30. If you have any questions, feel free to call a member of the survey team (Mr. Walter or Ms. Peterson) at ext. 777.

Your input is important to the organization. Thank you for your assistance.

Sincerely,

I. M. DaBoss
Chief Executive Officer

Figure 7.1. Sample Cover Letter for an Organizational Survey

repercussions because of their responses. It is always a good idea to emphasize that "Completion of this questionnaire is entirely voluntary."

▨ *Disinterest in or Discomfort With the Topic Area*

Respondents may choose not to respond or may not respond accurately if they are uncomfortable with or not interested in the survey topics. For example, men who receive a company sexual harassment survey may feel that the questions do not apply to them and, therefore, their input is not really needed and will not be missed. In this case, a good statement for the introduction would be, "Both women and men can experience sexual harassment. Please complete these questions, even if you have never experienced sexual harassment in this organization."

Respondents may fail to respond accurately if they are faced with personal questions, such as items asking about their home life. They may feel uncomfortable providing such information on an organizational survey. Therefore, the organization needs a very strong rationale (which should be made explicit in the introduction) for asking personal questions in a survey. "Just curious" is not good enough!

> ▩ Use a No. 2 pencil only.
>
> ▩ Erase completely any changes that you make.
>
> ▩ Make black marks that fill the circle.
>
> ▩ Do not make stray marks on the form.

Figure 7.2. Instructions for Use With Scannable Surveys

▩ *Evaluation Apprehension*

Respondents may be concerned about being singled out for possible evaluation, or they may think that the survey is actually a test that they can flunk. Where applicable, the introduction can include statements such as "This is not a test of your intelligence or ability. There are no right or wrong answers. Therefore, please answer all questions as honestly and accurately as possible."

Survey Instructions

To minimize confusion or misinterpretation, it is important that the survey items be preceded by a clear set of instructions. Like the survey items, the instructions should be written at the level of the respondents. General survey instructions should be given at the beginning of the survey, just after the introduction. These instructions should tell respondents what they are expected to do and how they should indicate their answers. For example, respondents might be told to "Carefully read each question and give your answer by marking the answer that best applies or by filling in the requested information."

Figure 7.2 shows some instructions that would be appropriate for a scannable survey.

If there is anything tricky, unusual, or potentially difficult about the survey, the general instructions should mention this. Instructions that apply only to certain survey questions need to be placed immediately preceding the questions to which they apply. For example, respondents should never be expected to remember a response scale. Instead, the scale should be provided on every page that contains items using that set of alternatives.

All instructions, both general and specific, should be easily distinguishable from the survey questions themselves. Putting instructions in boxes or using a different font style (e.g., bold, italics, or all caps) will focus readers' attention on the instructions.

After the instructions, it is a good idea to present one or more practice questions. Figure 7.3 provides an example. In our surveys, we fill in one or more of the practice questions to show people exactly how to complete each item. Although some readers may think this step is going overboard

---

Blacken the circle that corresponds to your answer.

My favorite color is:

○ Blue

● Red

○ Green

○ Pink

○ Other

Figure 7.3. Practice Question

on instructions, it is amazing how Murphy's Law affects surveys: What-ever can go wrong very often will!

The instructions are followed by the survey itself. At the end of the survey, respondents should be thanked for their participation and presented with brief instructions for returning the survey (e.g., mail back, drop in designated box, or return to survey administrator).

Pretesting the Survey

Before a major theatrical show opens on Broadway, it often plays to audiences in smaller cities. Reactions can be gauged and changes can be made before the actual opening night. Pretesting the survey serves a similar function. It offers the team a chance to see how the survey plays under realistic conditions, while allowing changes to be made. Once the survey content and length have been finalized, the team is ready to put the survey into its final administration format and test it under actual administration conditions.

Although most survey books view the pretest as an essential final step in the survey design process, this step is frequently neglected, rushed, sloppily done, or performed in a ritualistic manner (Converse & Presser, 1986; Dillman, 1978). After investing much time and effort into survey development, the team often wants to administer the instrument without going through one last tedious step. This false confidence or desire to complete the task is unfortunate because often the survey developers are too close to the survey to see what others may perceive as glaring problems with the instrument. The pretest presents a final chance to make sure that everything is ready to go.

In the pretest, feedback is obtained from organization members who are not on the survey team. Although pretest respondents need not be chosen by probability sampling, they should be obtained by something more than convenience samples (Sheatsley, 1983). Obtaining input from organization members in nearby offices may result in feedback from people who share many of the same characteristics and similar viewpoints as the survey developers. With such a sample, important concerns might not be raised during the evaluation of the survey. The survey team would be better served by using a diverse sample for pretesting. A concerted effort should be made to obtain respondents who reflect the characteristics of the final sample.

Verheyen (1988) suggests that survey pretesting be done with groups of 12 to 15 organization members. We prefer using 8 to 12 people per pretest group. This smaller size is easier to assemble, big enough to provide multiple viewpoints, and small enough to get everyone's comments in a relatively short period.

Pretesting the survey has two key objectives: evaluating the survey content and assessing the survey administration time.[3] The respondents should complete the survey under conditions that simulate as closely as possible the conditions that will be used during the actual survey administration. Before the pretest starts, participants should be informed of several things. These issues include that the purpose of the session is to evaluate the clarity of the introduction and instructions; the wording of items, response alternatives, and scales; and the comprehensiveness of the item alternatives. The participants should draw a circle around any instructions, items, or alternatives that were confusing, incomplete, or not applicable. Pretest participants should complete the survey at the speed that they would normally answer a questionnaire because the team is attempting to determine how long the average person takes to complete the survey.

After all the participants have completed the survey, a survey team member should interview or "debrief" the participants. This debriefing provides information on positive or negative attitudes toward the survey; instructions or items that were unclear, offensive, or difficult to understand or follow; and topics, items, or alternatives that should be added to the survey (Fowler, 1993; Howe & Gaeddert, 1991). What was clear to the survey team may not be readily apparent to organization members who did not develop the survey. This step will need to be repeated if major revisions are necessary after the initial pretest.

Because time is money on organizational surveys, the pretest should also be used to estimate the length of time it will take respondents to complete the survey. To facilitate the timing process, the survey team can include a final pretest item that asks the person to record the time in which he or she finished (Sheatsley, 1983). We have often been surprised by the length of time it takes people to complete our surveys.

At this point in the organizational survey process, the instrument still can be shortened, if necessary, to reach any previously agreed-on time limit for administration. Information about time is also important for determining the total cost of a survey. In the earlier phases of the survey planning, the team probably had to supply management with an estimate of the time and cost of the survey. The pretest acts as a check on the accuracy of the estimates. If the survey is going to take much longer for completion than was anticipated during the planning stage, the survey team should either shorten the survey or revise cost estimates and advise the appropriate personnel.

Obtaining Organizational Approval

The organizational survey team usually does not have the authority itself to conduct the survey. Typically, it must obtain approval from other organizational gatekeepers (Sieber, 1992). Because most survey teams do not include true power holders in the organizational hierarchy, they may find themselves at the mercy of other organizational players. To make matters worse, the goals and methods of these gatekeepers are not always in harmony. In obtaining organizational approval for the survey, three types of players—top management, unions, and institutional review boards—may play key roles.

Top Management

Higher-level management may have decided that a survey was needed, tasked personnel with getting the job done, and informally approved intermediate steps. Obtaining the final approval from this group may be an entirely different matter. In some organizations, the survey instrument may require that a number of managers sign off before the head of the organization gives final written approval. In addition to this process being time consuming, the survey team may face the practical challenge of having to change the survey to fit the specifications of authorities at various levels of management. At times, the changes desired by some gatekeepers may be contradictory to the modifications requested by others. Survey teams must be especially careful of the manager who wants changes (however well-meaning) that threaten the validity of the survey. In such a case, someone has to be able to say no.

One way to smooth over potential approval problems is to involve management as much and as soon as possible. Schiemann (1991) recommends that a senior member of the survey team consult on an ongoing basis with top management regarding the progress being made. We have had some success using such management points of contact. Typically, the point of contact acts as the survey team's representative with top management. At times, points of contact have almost become de facto members of our survey teams. In this way, management becomes committed to the success of the survey effort through involvement from the very beginning.

Unions

If the survey is to be administered to respondents who are members of a union, we advise that the input, and even the approval, of union representatives be sought. This input may be a requirement of the local labor-management agreement (Edwards & Thomas, 1993). In organizations where unions are important stake holders, the survey team should attempt to have the head of the union sign a cover letter endorsing the survey project. The success of the entire survey process can be endangered if word spreads that the union either is against the survey or views it as an attempt by management to manipulate or coerce employees.

We have found that unions are often initially suspicious of management-directed organizational surveys and may need to be persuaded that the goals of the survey are benign.[4] If the relationships between management and the organization's union(s) are characterized by an air of distrust, it is probably a good idea not to give the survey until relationships improve. Ideally, both the union and management should endorse the survey as a joint project. Attaining this goal, however, may be unrealistic in many organizational settings where surveys traditionally have been, and continue to be, under the direction and control of management.

Institutional Review Boards

An institutional review board (IRB) is usually composed of a number of individuals from differing backgrounds who determine whether a research project meets ethical standards (Giacalone & Rosenfeld, 1987). Although virtually all biomedical and social science research involving human participants is subject to IRB approval, IRBs are much less common in corporate settings—where most organizational surveys are conducted. Compared with survey teams conducting a similar project in a university or government setting where IRB approval is typically required, the survey team in an organizational setting often has an increased burden for ensuring that the rights of participants are protected (e.g., anonymity, confidentiality, lack of coercion). This burden may wax heavy because one of the principles of ethical research practice—that participation is voluntary and free of coercion—may be more difficult to guarantee in organizational surveys. In organizational settings, being asked by top management to complete a survey, especially if on-site administration is used, is an offer that is hard to refuse. Thus, many organizational surveys may have an element of implicit coercion.

If members of the survey team work at an institution that requires IRB approval, the initial reaction may be that such a requirement is a nuisance and is not really necessary. It must be remembered, however, that an IRB is usually the only impartial third party specifically concerned with protecting the rights of the participants. As such, the IRB's role is a necessary intrusion into the survey process. Our experience is that IRBs usually approve survey projects, even those that ask sensitive questions (e.g., sexual harassment, substance abuse). The key to obtaining IRB approval is to state clearly why the survey procedures are necessary and to demonstrate that care is taken to prevent respondents from experiencing improper coercion, risk, or harm as a consequence of their participation.

Preparing, Assembling, and Distributing the Survey Packet

Although obtaining approval may involve considerable effort, the real work begins after that step. Many of the activities (e.g., collating survey materials and mailing the survey packets) do not require high-level skills, but these tasks are critical to the efficient fielding of a survey. In some organizations, many of these tasks can be delegated to the organization's mailroom personnel or sent to a contractor, rather than carried out by members of the survey team. The tasks vary depending on the mode of survey administration. Because a mail-out survey is the most labor-intensive distribution method, it is used as a model for the following discussion.

Preparing the Contents of the Survey Packet

Typically, the survey itself is part of a larger survey packet. Depending on the type of survey administered, the survey packet could consist of various combinations of the following items: the survey (on paper or computer disk), a cover letter, a separate response sheet (for surveys using a generic scannable answer sheet), and a return envelope. The appropriate components would all be placed in an outer mailing envelope.

For mail-out surveys that will use the U.S. Postal Service, the survey team should provide postage-paid, preaddressed return envelopes. If business-reply mailing permits are used instead of stamps, the organization pays postage only on the surveys that are returned. Return envelopes are not usually needed with group administration. If the survey is being sent and returned via the organization's internal mail system, interoffice mail envelopes can be used for survey returns and probably do not have to be provided to respondents.

When surveys are mailed to respondents' homes, outer mailing envelopes must include the respondent's name and address. If the surveys are distributed internally, each mailing envelope must have the respondent's name and department. In either case, the addressing can be done most efficiently using computer-generated mailing labels.

The survey team needs to prepare a survey package for each potential respondent. If new copies of the survey are to be sent out in follow-up mailings or if potential respondents misplace their surveys and want a replacement, additional survey packages should be readily available. Our advice is to have extras of all supplies handy.

Occasionally, more than one form of a paper survey is administered. In addition to a core set of items relevant to everyone, an organization may need different types of information from various subgroups (e.g., managers vs. clerical staff vs. production workers). If a large number of items needs to be tailored to specific subgroups, it may be too costly to print all subgroup-specific questions on every survey. Moreover, multiple branching points can be confusing.

When multiple versions of a survey (or even several different surveys being distributed in the same time frame) are administered, the survey should contain an identifier that makes the versions easy to distinguish.

Our preference is to color code different survey versions. For example, managers might receive a survey on white paper, whereas the survey directed to clerical staff is copied onto blue paper. Such color coding can be done on any type of paper-and-pencil survey—traditional, generic scanner sheets, or customized scannable forms—as well as on computerized surveys by using colored diskette labels. When surveys are returned, color coding speeds the initial processing and makes it less likely that different versions of the same survey will be confused with each other.

Distributing the Survey Through the Mail

With group administration, the process of survey distribution—getting the surveys to and from the respondents—is relatively straightforward. Distribution is more complex when the instruments must be delivered through the U.S. Postal Service or interoffice mail.

▩ *Distributing Surveys Through the U.S. Postal Service*

In a mail-out survey, respondents receive the survey packet at their office or home address. Every effort should be made to avoid mailing during the holiday season (Thanksgiving Day through New Year's Day) because the mail delivery and return may be slower than usual and respondents may be away or otherwise busy for an extended period. If the mailing uses the U.S. Postal Service, materials may be sent either bulk rate or first class. Although first-class postage should ensure that mail is forwarded, it is our experience that the postal service does not always send large first-class envelopes to the next address. Thus, some preliminary work is needed to ensure that the address list for the survey is as accurate as possible.

In one of our organizational surveys for the military, about 10% of the 10,000 originally sent surveys were returned because the mailing addresses were incorrect. This problem should be less severe for civilian organizations because members of those organizations move less frequently than military personnel. Organizations such as universities, however, may have even poorer home address records for groups such as alumni and alumnae. To avoid or minimize this problem, some organizations use a *prenotification letter*. The prenotification letter will be forwarded to a new address if the new address is less than a year old. The letter can request that the respondent look at the address on the envelope and send any corrections to the survey team.[5]

▩ *Distributing Surveys Through Interoffice Mail*

If all the personnel to be surveyed are located at sites that receive interoffice mail, it may be desirable to send the surveys out in this way. A major advantage of the interoffice mail survey is that it entails little or no mailing costs.

▩ *Other Delivery Methods*

If all the personnel are located in a single site or at relatively few locations, it may be possible to distribute the surveys by hand to individual respondents or to groups of individuals. The hand-delivery process can be done by giving each supervisor (or a designated point of contact) a survey for each person in his or her group and asking that the supervisor deliver a survey to each subordinate. Alternatively, a member of the survey team can personally hand a survey to each potential respondent. The respondents can return their surveys either to a central location (e.g., a locked survey box outside the cafeteria) to promote anonymity or directly to the person who gave them the survey. In the latter case, envelopes that can be sealed should be provided.

Notes

1. Some authors (e.g., Bourque & Clark, 1992) distinguish between two types of preadministration tests of surveys. Bourque and Clark (1992) view pretesting as "testing parts of [the] data collection instruments and procedures" (p. 32). This task can be performed with focus groups, in the field, or in a laboratory. Pilot testing, on the other hand, occurs when the survey content has been finalized. During pilot testing, the survey team attempts to simulate the conditions that will occur when the actual survey is fielded. Because both steps are often mixed in practice and other authors do not make the pretest-pilot test distinction, we use the term *pretest* to refer to the entire preadministration testing process.

2. The organization's commitment to the survey process conveyed in the cover letter can be reinforced by including publicity about the survey in the company newsletter.

3. Verheyen (1988) notes another benefit that can be derived from the survey pretesting. The data obtained during the pretest can be used to design and test statistical analysis programs. The programs can be written and debugged while awaiting the data from the survey administration. This advanced planning and work allows the survey team to begin analyses as soon as the complete database is available. This may prove particularly useful if the survey team is being squeezed by management to provide quick results.

4. During the late 1950s, some companies used surveys to help them keep labor unions out of their organizations. The companywide surveys were used to determine whether employees were dissatisfied enough that they might form unions or engage in union-based threats against the organization (Barmash, 1993).

5. The U.S. Postal Service gives a discount for large mailings that have letters bundled by zip code. Although this procedure can be done by hand, it is very time consuming and inefficient for large surveys. The survey team may want to check with the mail department to determine if the organization owns Group 1 computer software. This software sorts addresses by zip codes, adds the last four digits of the nine-digit zip code, adds bar coding, and does a cursory examination of the addresses for completeness. The U.S. Postal Service can supply additional details on both bulk-mailing regulations and this software. Survey teams in countries outside the United States need to familiarize themselves with their local postal regulations and practices before conducting mail-out surveys.

Monitoring and Maximizing Response Rates

8

One of the biggest problems facing those who conduct organizational surveys is getting people to participate once they have been selected. People may hang up when contacted for a telephone interview survey about voting preferences or refuse to be interviewed for a marketing survey when approached in a shopping mall. For organizational surveys, the problem of how many people participate is most frequently encountered when the surveys are distributed by mail. Individuals who get a survey in company mail may add the survey to their "to do" lists and never get it done. Those who receive surveys through the U.S. Postal Service may trash them as junk mail.

If a large percentage of the potential respondents elect not to complete their surveys, all the time, effort, and expense involved in conducting a survey may be wasted. Thus, it is in the survey team's best interests to monitor the return of surveys carefully once the questionnaires are in the field and to take steps that maximize the number that come back.

Monitoring Response Rates

The percentage of people who complete and return a survey is referred to as the *response rate*.[1] As we mention in Chapter 11, it is standard practice to indicate the response rate, whether in an oral presentation to top management or in a written report that will be distributed throughout the organization. Survey teams and sponsors use the response rate as a quality indicator for judging how successful the survey administration was.[2] As Mangione (1995) notes, "low response rates give the appearance of a poor quality study and shake the consumer's confidence in the results of the study. The study becomes less useful or less influential because it does not have the trappings of quality" (p. 62). Thus, the general rule is simple but essential: The higher the response rate, the better!

TABLE 8.1 How to Calculate a Response Rate

Number of surveys mailed:	1,000
Number of surveys not delivered:	50
Number of completed surveys:	565

1,000 (total surveys mailed) – 50 (undeliverable) = 950

565 / 950 = .59

.59 × 100 = 59% (Response Rate)

Calculating Response Rates

The response rate is the number of people from whom surveys were received divided by the number of people to whom the survey was mailed. If surveys are returned by the post office as undeliverable because of incorrect mailing addresses or because respondents could not be located (e.g., they moved and left no forwarding address), these surveys should be subtracted from the mailed-to number when the response rate is calculated. Because response rates are conventionally given as percentages, the last step in this process is to multiply the resulting fraction by 100.

Table 8.1 shows how the response rate would be calculated for a survey that was mailed to the home addresses of 1,000 organization members.

What Is an Acceptable Response Rate?

Although there is no "magic" number that establishes a "good" response rate, any organizational survey should have a target response rate of at least 50%. Babbie (1973) indicates that a response rate of 50% or greater is adequate, a response rate of 60% is good, and a rate of 70% or more is very good.

Most response rates reported in the published research literature range from 35% to 80%. One review (Heberlein & Baumgartner, 1978) used a statistical technique called *meta-analysis* to compare survey response rates obtained in many different studies. Heberlein and Baumgartner (1978) found that the average response rates were 46% for single-mailing surveys (no follow-up or precontact), 68% for surveys with one follow-up, and 61% for all the surveys studied. Another meta-analysis (Church, 1993) found an average response rate of 49% for surveys that used incentives and 36% for surveys that did not use incentives.

Nonresponse Bias

Why is it so important that a reasonably high response rate be achieved? First, if a sample is being used, the sample size may need to be expanded if the survey team has reason to anticipate a low response rate for the current survey (e.g., based on low response rates on similar past surveys). This lower response rate translates into a higher cost for survey materials, labor, and the like. Second, a small response rate could produce insufficient data for analysis or conclusions. This problem may be especially vexing if the survey team wants to conduct analyses comparing the responses of subgroups such as men versus women or blue-collar versus white-collar employees. Third, the survey team cannot simply assume that nonrespondents would have answered the survey questions in the same manner as respondents did (General Accounting Office, 1992).

When nonrespondents are systematically different from respondents, *nonresponse bias* is present. Nonresponse bias can severely limit the generalizability of the survey findings. When the percentage of nonrespondents is low (i.e., the response rate is high), nonresponse bias is less of a problem. In this case, even if nonrespondents do differ dramatically from those who completed the survey, their absence should not affect the overall survey results or conclusions very much. When the response rate is low, however, the possibility that the views held by those who did not respond are systematically different from those who returned the survey may degrade the quality of the findings, conclusions, and recommendations.

In what ways are respondents likely to differ from nonrespondents? First, people who have a particular interest in the subject matter of the survey may be more likely to return the survey than organization members who are less interested (see Fowler, 1993). Second, individuals who are relatively more literate and educated are more likely to return a survey than those who are less literate (Bradburn & Sudman, 1988). Consequently, an organizational survey having a low response rate might result in biased findings. In such an instance, the findings and conclusions would give undue weight to the most educated and interested segments of the sample—those individuals who returned their surveys at higher than normal rates.

The following example illustrates the concerns that nonresponse bias introduces. An organization decided to survey its staff about its current performance awards system. The response rate for the survey was 30%. Of those who responded, 90% were satisfied with the system. With such a high rate of satisfaction, a decision was made to make no changes to the system.

Nonresponse bias may have led to an erroneous conclusion that the vast majority of employees were satisfied with the organization's performance awards system. That decision failed to take into account the opinions of the 70% of employees who received a survey but did not respond. Some of those people might never have gotten a performance award and chose not to respond out of bitterness or indifference. Other employees might have believed that surveys never lead to change, and therefore threw their surveys away. Other employees may not have returned surveys because they did not trust the survey team's assurances of anonymity. In sum, it is possible that a high percentage of these nonrespondents were dissatisfied with the current system.

Dealing With Nonresponse Bias

In situations where nonresponse bias is a possibility, the team needs to determine the extent to which survey findings are influenced by the differential return of surveys. A common way to address nonresponse bias is to compare key demographic characteristics of respondents to the demographics of the population. In the example described above, the survey team could have compared the respondents to the overall employee population on demographic (such as education level, race, gender, and age) and organizational variables (such as job type, salary level, department, and tenure with the organization). It is reassuring if the responding sample closely matches the population on all these variables, although it does not guarantee that there is no nonresponse bias. On the other hand, if the respondents are different on one or several of these variables, then nonresponse bias could be a problem, and the survey findings cannot be safely generalized to the population of employees.

Another alternative for dealing with nonresponse bias is to compare respondents with nonrespondents on key demographic variables. This requires that the identities of the survey respondents be known, which can be accomplished by asking respondents for identifying information or embedding an identification code in the survey. The statistical comparisons of demographic and organizational variables described above can then be made between respondents and nonrespondents. When the two groups are similar on known demographic variables, it is less likely that the respondents and nonrespondents will have different survey response patterns. That possibility cannot, however, be entirely ruled out (General Accounting Office, 1992).

A third, more labor-intensive, approach requires that the survey team attempt to contact and interview a sample of nonrespondents (General Accounting Office, 1992). The contacted nonrespondents are interviewed (usually by telephone), and their responses to a number of key survey items are sought. These responses are compared with the answers obtained from individuals who returned the original survey. If the groups do not differ, the survey team can breathe a sigh of relief and base its conclusions on the data obtained from respondents. If the groups differ systematically, however, this limitation regarding the findings and conclusions must be noted in the oral and written presentations of the survey results.

Ways to Maximize Response Rates

The best way to avoid the possible problems that accompany nonresponse bias is to take proactive steps to maximize the percentage of surveys returned. In this section, we describe several techniques that have been developed and studied by survey researchers. Many of these techniques are listed in Table 8.2.

Prenotification: The Survey Is Coming! The Survey Is Coming!

Some teams contact potential respondents before mailing the actual survey. This type of initial contact is called *prenotification*. A letter or postcard is usually used to inform organization members that they have been chosen to participate in the survey, to describe the topic areas and objectives of the survey, and to include a high-level person's strongly worded request for participation and return of the survey (Coffey, 1993).

TABLE 8.2 Techniques to Increase Survey Response Rates

Factors Found to Increase Survey Response Rates

▨ Repeated contact: the most important factor in increasing response rates

▨ Survey follow-ups by mail, phone, or in person

▨ Incentives

▨ Prenotification

▨ Inclusion of return postage

▨ Using first-class postage on the return envelope (rather than business reply postage)

▨ Importance of the survey and saliency of survey topics

▨ Ordering survey topics to match the priorities of respondents (with the most important topics appearing first)

Factors That May Increase Survey Response Rates

▨ Cover letters that use appeals from high-level sponsors (e.g., a letter from company president)

▨ Personalization of surveys

▨ Inclusion of return envelopes

▨ Using special delivery or certified mail for follow-ups

▨ Survey length: shorter (vs. longer) survey length associated with higher response rates

Factors That Have Little Effect on Response Rates

▨ Whether new copies of the survey are mailed with follow-up reminders

▨ Postcard vs. letter follow-ups

▨ Whether surveys are mailed first or third class

▨ Whether or not respondents are given deadlines

▨ Whether or not computerized answer sheets are used

In addition to getting the potential respondent ready to participate, the prenotification can be used to solicit address updates. Large organizations such as the military (where personnel move often) find this additional function of prenotification to be extremely useful. Prenotification may be similarly useful to loose-knit organizations such as alumni/alumnae associations that have only infrequent contact with their members.

Follow-Up Until You Drop The single most important factor in obtaining a good response rate is making repeated contacts with nonrespondents (Fowler, 1993; Heberlein & Baumgartner, 1978; Mangione, 1995). Follow-ups can be as simple as a postcard sent to all members of the sample reminding them to return the survey if they have not already done so and thanking them if they have sent it in.

Alternatively, follow-up techniques can be used to target nonrespondents only. New survey packages can be sent just to nonrespondents with a reminder letter or note. Telephone calls can be made telling nonrespondents that their completed surveys are needed. Whether written or oral, the follow-ups should be brief and friendly in tone. The follow-ups should convey the idea that each respondent's input is desired and needed. They should either include another copy of the survey or list a telephone number so that those who have not yet returned the survey can request another one. Some survey professionals use humor in their follow-up postcards or letters. Our favorite is the survey team that sent a letter with a large picture of a rhinoceros that began, "We've considered the possibility that a rampaging rhino has eaten your questionnaire . . ." (Berdie et al., 1986, p. 298).

▪ *How Many Follow-Ups Are Needed?*

A meta-analysis (Heberlein & Baumgartner, 1978) examined the relationship between the number of survey follow-ups and response rate. The researchers estimated that the first follow-up mailing nets a return of about 20% of the initial mailing, a second follow-up yields about 12% more, and a third follow-up yields about 10%. Additional follow-ups beyond the third seem to add only negligibly to the overall response rate, and they also represent an annoyance factor that may hamper future survey efforts.[3] Babbie (1973) reports a similar pattern. He found that 40% of surveys are typically returned as a result of the initial mailing. An additional 20% are returned after the first follow-up, and an additional 10% are returned after the second follow-up. Mangione (1995) notes that a first survey follow-up typically yields a response rate that is about half the rate obtained from the initial survey mailing.

The number of follow-up mailings needed to obtain a respectable response rate depends largely on the initial response rate. If the response rate within a few weeks of the initial mailing is 60%, the survey team can generally expect that one follow-up mailing will increase the response rate to between 70% and 80%. If this level of response is deemed adequate for the survey team's purposes (and it should be for most organizational surveys), then one follow-up mailing will be sufficient. If, on the other hand, the initial mailing yields a response rate of only 30%, two or more follow-ups may be necessary.

▪ *When Should Follow-Up Reminders Be Sent?*

Most survey researchers consider 10 days to 3 weeks to be a reasonable interval between mailings. Babbie (1973) reports that his research office spaced the mailings about 2 to 3 weeks apart. Mangione (1995) recommends that the first reminders be sent about 2 weeks after the initial mailing. Other survey specialists send follow-ups when replies from earlier mailings have dwindled considerably. Dillman (1978) suggests sending a follow-up postcard about 10 days after the initial mailing and a second reminder with a copy of the survey 10 days after the first follow-up.

Potential respondents may perceive a reminder sent too soon after the initial mailing to be annoying. Even worse, the reminder card may reach respondents before they have received the actual survey. During one of our worldwide organizational surveys, questionnaires were mailed at bulk rate (to save thousands of dollars), and many arrived after the first-class reminder postcards had been received. (We got lots of nasty phone calls!)

■ *Targeting Nonrespondents Using Postcards*

For anonymous surveys, we typically send one or two follow-up postcards to all members of the sample. We are always surprised at how many people do not read the postcard carefully. Many respondents call to inform us that they have returned their survey and could we please check to make sure that their survey had been received. We patiently explain that the survey is anonymous so it would be impossible for us to locate an individual's survey, thank them for participating, and promise ourselves that next time reminders will be sent only to those who did not return surveys.

Even with anonymous mail-back surveys, the postcard technique makes it possible to employ follow-up procedures that target only nonrespondents. One side of the postcard has the survey team's address and the other side has a mailing label with the person's name and address. In the survey instructions, the respondent is asked to mail the completed survey and postcard at the same time, but separately. Thus, the survey team gets two separate pieces of mail, a postcard and a survey, from each person. This process allows the survey team to determine who the nonrespondents are so they can be targeted for follow-up mailings. At the same time, the people from whom completed surveys have been received have their sense of anonymity maintained and are not bothered by reminder notices.

If surveys are not anonymous, it is easy to send follow-ups to nonrespondents only. Respondent names are simply checked off a master list when their completed surveys are received. Follow-ups are then sent to nonrespondents. If the survey team does not want to use respondents' names, an identification number can be written or printed on each survey and return envelope. If confidential identification is being used, the cover letter should explain that the number is being used only to track survey completion. We have found that when no explanation is given, people may become suspicious. Consequently, some potential respondents may refuse to complete the survey, and others may return it with the number blackened out or ripped off.

If They Won't Respond, Bribe Them

Incentives seem to have a substantial effect on response rates, increasing them by as much as 25% (Yammarino, Skinner, & Childers, 1991). Because of this, incentives such as money, lottery tickets, or prizes have become popular features of many mail-back surveys. One of us received a marketing survey in the mail with a $1 bill enclosed. *USA Today* (Parker, 1993) reports that a consumer-research business sent out more than $300,000 in single dollar bills to individuals who received its surveys. Apparently, the company felt the cost was justified given the 5% increase in response rates associated with the dollar incentives.

Surprisingly, even small amounts of money can produce large increases in response rates. Incentives as small as 25 cents have been found to increase response rates significantly (James & Bolstein, 1990). Also, monetary incentives enclosed with the survey seem to have a much greater effect than monetary rewards that depend on return of the survey (Church, 1993). Nonmonetary response incentives (such as lottery tickets and pens) also tend to increase response rates, provided they are enclosed with the survey.

Futrell (1994) suggests that small incentives increase response rates not because of their reward value but because they make potential respondents feel guilty about taking something without returning the survey. Regardless of why incentives work, considering the costs incurred by nonresponse (e.g., extra mailing and printing) and the effect of a low response rate on data quality, it may be cost-effective for the survey team to include incentives.[4]

Incentives may have less practical applications for organizational surveys administered to employees. The incentive or guilt that spurs an individual to return a survey from a car dealership may lose its effect in organizations that survey their employees every 6 months or annually. Additionally, the possibility exists that if incentives are offered for one organizational survey, people may expect greater incentives for completing future surveys.

Make the Survey Meaningful

Survey salience is the degree to which the survey deals with topics that are relevant and important to respondents. People are more likely to complete and return a survey that they find meaningful and relevant than one that they find trivial and unimportant. Heberlein and Baumgartner (1978) found a 77% response rate for salient surveys and a 42% response rate for nonsalient surveys.

In organizational settings, the survey team may or may not be able to control survey salience because the choice of topics is often dictated from upper management or by a particular organizational problem. The team may, however, be able to increase survey salience by adding items of interest to respondents. At least some of these items should be placed at the beginning of the survey so that people's interest and attention are captured.

An especially thorny problem occurs if the survey is more salient for members of one subgroup than for other respondents. For example, a sexual harassment survey would likely be of greater interest to women than men. If this greater survey salience is translated into a markedly higher response rate for women than for men, the harassment rates calculated for men would be based on a much lower response rate. The team could minimize the effect of different salience levels on response rates by including some general interest items regarding views of the organization or job satisfaction at the beginning of the survey.

It's as Easy as TDM

Dillman (1978) advocates a set of procedures called the Total Design Method (TDM), specifically aimed at producing very high response rates. He claims that TDM has never obtained a response rate below 60% and that the average is a 77% response rate (Dillman, 1985). This figure may be lower; we have noticed a dramatic decrease in response rates to mail-back surveys in the past 5 years.

TDM involves numerous procedures for survey construction, administration, and follow-up. These procedures include having the researchers personally sign each cover letter, personalizing the survey materials (e.g., using actual names such as "Dear Walt" or "Dear Mr. Peterson" rather than the generic "Dear Respondent"), using first-class postage, making follow-up contacts (possibly with certified mail), and adhering to a precise schedule of mail-out and follow-up dates.

It remains to be seen how much general applicability each TDM step and other general purpose survey procedures have for the differing circumstances involved in organizational surveys.

What Works: A Summary

Several meta-analyses summarize the research on techniques for increasing survey response rates. Yammarino et al. (1991) found the following factors to be significant across studies: monetary incentives of 50 cents or less or $1.00 or more, a cover letter that uses appeals, inclusion of a return envelope, inclusion of postage, and survey length (fewer than 4 pages was better). The other factors that significantly affected response rates were prenotification and repeated contacts. Similarly, Fox, Crask, and Kim (1988) did a meta-analysis of factors potentially associated with higher response rates to mail-out surveys. Prenotification, follow-ups, stamped return postage, sponsorship, and monetary incentives were found to enhance response rates significantly. Another meta-analysis (Heberlein & Baumgartner, 1978) found significant effects of repeated contacts and survey salience. Length of survey did not have a simple effect on response rate, although longer length was associated with a lower response rate when survey salience and number of contacts were statistically controlled. A meta-analysis that focused specifically on the type of postage used on the return envelopes (Armstrong & Lusk, 1987) found that first-class postage on return envelopes yields a higher response rate than business reply postage, with an average response rate gain (across 20 studies) of 9%.

Practical Suggestions for Increasing Response Rates

We close this chapter with a list of practical suggestions for maximizing the chance that surveys will be sent to the intended respondents and that those people will complete and return the surveys. These suggestions are found in Table 8.3. Survey teams are cautioned that many of the sugges-

TABLE 8.3 Practical Suggestions for Increasing Response Rates of Mail-Out Surveys

▪ Have an up-to-date address list so all potential respondents can be contacted.

▪ Include a cover letter with purposes of the survey and appeals to complete it.

▪ Make sure respondents know that their help is important; explain how their help will be useful.

▪ Make it clear how the respondent will ultimately benefit.

▪ Make sure respondents are not threatened by the survey or the uses to which the data will be put.

▪ Explain that their data will be kept confidential and will never be reported except in aggregate form.

▪ Use incentives.

▪ Keep the survey short (e.g., 4 pages or fewer) when possible.

▪ Don't let the survey jump from topic to topic in an illogical fashion.

▪ Minimize open-ended questions. Remember that it is a survey, not an essay exam.

▪ Order the survey with the questions of most importance to respondents at the beginning, moderately important questions in the middle, and least important questions at the end.

▪ Include a stamped, preaddressed return envelope for mail-back surveys.

▪ Send follow-up postcards or letters reminding respondents to complete the survey. Emphasize the importance of the study and the need for a high rate of response.

▪ Send follow-ups only to nonrespondents, if possible. If this cannot be done (e.g., for anonymous surveys), follow-ups should be sent to all respondents in the original sample. Those who already returned the survey are thanked; those who have not are asked to complete it.

tions were developed from research with nonorganizational surveys. We cannot vouch for the applicability of all the suggestions to organizational settings.

Notes

1. Some percentage of individuals usually return the survey but leave some or all the items unanswered. We discuss this issue in Chapter 9 in the section on missing data.

2. Survey teams may indirectly cause overall response rates to be lower or higher if they use disproportionate stratified sampling (see Chapter 5) to ensure that enough respondents in certain subgroups will be available for analysis. If the individuals in the group that is oversampled are less likely to respond (e.g., those with less education or entry-level workers) than the rest of the sample, the overall response rate will be lower than if a simple random sample had been used. The opposite is true if the oversampled group has a higher response rate (e.g., supervisors) than the rest of the sample. In these instances, it may be appropriate to report response rates for specific subgroups in addition to reporting the rate for the whole sample.

3. The concern over the future consequences of annoying potential respondents through repeated contacts is more of a worry for organizations that routinely survey their employees than for those who conduct marketing or public opinion surveys with the general population. This frustration factor has less effect on these latter types of surveys because the respondents in surveys of the general population are typically one-time participants or are paid to provide survey information.

4. A combination of incentives and repeated contacts has been more effective in increasing response rates than either technique used alone. Therefore, a survey with follow-ups and an incentive can be expected to produce a higher response rate than a one-contact survey with no incentive (James & Bolstein, 1990).

Data Processing

9

The survey has been administered and completed by a satisfactory number of respondents. This chapter describes the tasks and procedures that bridge the gap between survey administration and data analysis. These tasks include coding closed- and open-ended survey responses so that they are in a form that can be entered into the computer and are suitable for subsequent data analyses. In addition, decisions must be made about handling missing data. Many of these tasks can be planned and even completed while the survey is in the field.

To facilitate the subsequent analysis of the data, the survey team needs to prepare a *codebook*. A codebook documents the decisions used to code data and prepare the survey data file. At minimum, the codebook should contain a copy of the survey that has each question annotated with its variable name and the codes used to represent possible responses. The codebook should also have a listing of the length and location of the variables in the data file. Although the codebook is useful to people entering the data, it may also prove extremely important at a later date. For example, further analyses may be needed some time after the data coder has left the organization, or so much time has passed that the survey team cannot depend on its collective memory to say precisely what was done.

We describe in this chapter some of the most common decisions faced in the data-handling phase of the survey process. Readers who desire additional in-depth information on data coding and processing are referred to Bourque and Clark (1992).

Preparing for Data Entry: Data Coding for Closed-Ended Questions

Before any analyses can take place, survey responses must be translated to a format that can be read by a computer (Karweit & Meyers, 1983). Data coding involves naming variables, assigning values to item response categories, and determining the layout of the data file. If the survey has been carefully constructed and consists mostly of closed-ended questions, data coding is fairly straightforward. Coding for closed-ended questions can begin before a single completed survey is returned. Coding of open-ended responses, which is a more complicated procedure, can occur only after completed surveys are available. Therefore, open-ended response coding is discussed separately in the last section of this chapter.

Naming and Labeling Variables

Each survey question is represented in the data file by one or more variables. The variable's name is a shorthand way of referring to an item. Some variable names are obvious, such as GENDER for the gender of the respondent. In other cases, a short variable name must represent a much more complex piece of information. For example, the item "How satisfied are you with Organization X's health benefits?" might be assigned the variable name HEALTH.

The length (i.e., the maximum number of characters allowed) and form (i.e., what characters are permitted) of the variable name depend on the computer program used to analyze the data. For example, most of the standard statistical analysis programs (e.g., SPSS, SAS, BMDP) allow a maximum of 8 characters for a variable name. This limitation may force the survey team to give the variable a title such as Q31G to indicate that the responses are for item G on question 31. The meaningfulness of this variable name can be enhanced with variable labels.

SPSS-X, SAS, and BMDP allow a longer label to be assigned to a variable name. In most cases, the variable label can be up to 40 characters long and appears with the variable name on computer printouts. Sometimes, the full wording of short items can be used as variable labels. Although typing labels is time consuming and boring, it makes reading and interpreting analysis printouts much easier, especially if there is a need to revisit survey results at a later time.

The first variable name in the codebook should be ID (or something similar) to represent each returned survey. An identification number can be written or stamped on anonymous surveys in the order they are returned. Surveys administered under either confidential or identified conditions should have an identification number printed on them before administration. Optically scanned paper surveys are usually assigned an identification number automatically when passed through the scanner. This feature is also available in some computer-administered survey software (e.g., Sawtooth's Ci3). An identification number makes it easier to correct errors when the data file is cleaned.

Assigning Values to Responses

The process of assigning value labels to the data during the construction and printing of the survey is called *precoding* (Bourque & Clark, 1992). When the survey is precoded with the values for each answer printed on the survey, data coding and entry are quicker and easier.

▦ *Variables Requiring Numerical Responses*

Some item values are entered verbatim into the computer in the numerical form provided by the respondent. Variables that fall into this category are answers such as ratings or fill-in-the-blank responses indicating a quantity.

For example, an item from an employee attitude survey on car-pooling might ask, "How long (in minutes) is your typical, daily, one-way commute to work?" The respondent's answer, 15 minutes, can be entered directly into the computer as "15." Similarly, the coding for a 5-point Likert scale would be provided automatically by a respondent's rating (e.g., 1 = Strongly disagree, 2 = Disagree, 3 = Neither agree nor disagree, 4 = Agree, 5 = Strongly agree).

Just as variables can be given extended labels, statistical software often allows the inclusion of value labels. In the Likert scale example, labels (such as "Strongly agree") can be associated with each numeric code. These labels appear on printouts, making them easier to read and interpret.

▨ *Variables Requiring Alphabetic Responses*

Other types of responses need to be translated for computer entry. In general, these variables involve qualitative answers that are supplied to multiple-choice, yes-no, true-false, and other such questions. With rare exceptions (e.g., respondent name in identified surveys), all closed-ended responses should be coded as numbers. Responses to the variable GENDER, for example, should be recorded in the data file as 1 for Male and 2 for Female (rather than M and F).

This general convention is used for several reasons. First, if data are entered directly from paper into a computer file, entering only numbers speeds data entry—the numeric key pad portion of the keyboard can be used for all data entry. Using only the number pad also lessens the likelihood of data entry errors because it eliminates switching back and forth between the regular keyboard (for letters) and the number pad. Second, when looking at the data file for possible errors, it is often difficult to spot a letter "O" that is supposed to be the number 0 or the letter "l" that should have been the number 1. Even though these pairs of characters look virtually the same, each character is stored very differently by the computer. Statistical programs get the computer equivalent of heartburn if they are told that the values being entered are numeric and an alphabetic value is found. Third, creation of new variables (e.g., a job satisfaction scale) from two or more survey variables is greatly simplified if all the variables are numbers.

▨ *Consistency in Assigning Values*

It is a good idea to maintain consistency in coding when different items use the same response alternatives. For example, 1 might always be used for Yes and 2 might always be used for No. Such consistency makes it easier to interpret the survey results during the data analysis phase.

Designating Code(s) for Missing Values

An important decision the survey team must face is about how the data entry personnel will indicate that a respondent did not supply an answer. At the data-coding stage, this procedure should be kept very simple to avoid confusion. Therefore, the survey team should use the same code for all variables, if possible.

In many situations, we leave blank spaces to indicate when a value is missing. Others prefer to use a number to represent a missing data point. For example, if answers to an item can range from 1 to 5, a 9 could be used as the missing value indicator. Care must be exercised when assigning numbers as missing responses; these values may accidentally be read into the computer as real values during statistical analyses. Finally, some people prefer to enter missing data as a period (.); this strategy minimizes hand movements and allows all numeric and missing responses to be entered from the number pad. Relative to using a space for missing value coding, use of the period has the added advantage of helping the data cleaner count columns when checking for mistakes.

Entering Data

The results of a meticulously designed and administered organizational survey can be compromised by sloppy data entry. Babbie (1973) notes that " 'dirty' data will almost always produce misleading research findings" (p. 202). Although tedious, accurately entering data is a vital part of the survey process. During this phase, the survey team must vigilantly guard against errors entering the data file and take steps to detect and correct data entry procedures that increase the odds of errors. If members of the survey team are advocates of the total quality or zero defects management philosophies, this is the stage where they can practice what they preach.

Data File Organization

All survey responses need to be entered into a data file. In a rectangular data file (the type of file we most often use), the horizontal lines or rows represent data from each survey respondent, and the vertical lines or columns of data represent the values for the variables (Bourque & Clark, 1992). The data from one survey respondent make up one or more records, and each survey item is a variable assigned a location in the file.

The data for a record can be entered in either fixed or free fields. In a *fixed-field data file,* each variable is recorded in the same location on each record. In a *free-field data file,* the variables are recorded in the same order for each record, but not necessarily in the same column locations; values are separated by blanks or commas. We prefer a fixed-field data file because it makes checking data quality much easier. In either case, it is a good idea to code the data in the same order as the items appear on the survey (Fowler, 1988).

Assigning column locations to variables can be done while the survey is in the field and should be part of the codebook. This procedure can be trickier than it looks. More than once, we have designed a coding scheme and later discovered that a variable had more digits than anticipated. It is better to overestimate the number of columns needed than to underestimate. For example, for annual salary, the survey team might allow six columns. If the largest salary in the sample needs only five columns, the extra blank column does not cause a problem.

Because the actual process of data entry varies greatly by method of administration, the remainder of this section is organized according to administration modes.

Data Entry for Computerized and Scannable Surveys

If the survey was administered by computer or completed on scanner forms, the great advantages of these techniques now become apparent: Data entry is either already completed (in the case of computer) or is automated (for scanner surveys). In both these instances, data exist in a form the computer can already understand (Karweit & Meyers, 1983). *Source data entry* has the advantage of eliminating coding and data entry errors while cutting costs and humanpower required to do the data entry. These benefits may be offset, however, by the requirement for additional, often expensive, computer and scanner equipment.

Manual Data Entry

When surveys are administered without the aid of scannable answer sheets or a computer, the respondents' answers require *transcriptive data entry.* That is, data must be coded and entered into the computer manually (Karweit & Meyers, 1983). At least two major decisions face the survey team regarding how these data are to be entered. Who should enter the data? What data software should be used?

▦ *Who Should Enter the Data*

Using members of the survey team to enter data has the advantage of limiting the number of people in the organization who see individual survey responses. Data entry by the survey team may not, however, be a cost-effective use of human resources. Survey team members are often paid more per hour than data entry personnel, and the team members probably enter fewer characters per minute than professional data entry personnel would.

Given that data-processing professionals usually enter data more quickly and accurately than survey team members, other issues need to be considered to determine whether the data entry personnel should be employed in-house or on contract. If the surveys contain confidential information or information that is in any way damaging to the organization, the organization should probably elect to perform the processing in-house. On the other hand, if these concerns are minimal, the organization might decide to contract out the data entry. Similarly, the organization might decide to contract for these services if the survey team is afraid that internal data entry professionals might be able to identify specific respondents by their demographics.

▦ *What Software Should Be Used for Data Entry*

Choosing a database program may become an issue when the survey team decides to enter the data itself. In other cases, the data entry professionals (both in-house and external) will already have selected the software. Regardless of the software used, the data-processing professionals should be able to deliver a data file that is readable by the computer and statistical software that will be used for data cleaning and analyses.

Many database programs (e.g., FoxPro, dBase, or Paradox) and other software (e.g., Teleform for Windows) can be used to develop a data entry form. To facilitate data entry further, some programs can be used to create forms that look like the survey instrument itself. With these latter types of programs, the variable to be entered appears on the screen, which lessens the chances of entering data for the wrong variable.

These specialized data entry forms have a number of advantages. Entering data using a data entry form is typically much easier and straightforward than entering the data directly into a generic data file. Also, the software can be programmed to include validity checks. For example, these checking procedures look for common input errors and reject out-of-bounds values. A disadvantage is that these software programs require either prior experience or some learning time built into the survey cycle. Similarly, designing the data entry form may be time consuming. A third disadvantage is that after data are entered, the data file has to be imported into a statistical package for analysis. This highlights an advantage of using statistical packages that have a data entry option, such as the Windows version of SPSS.

Another possibility for data entry is the use of a spreadsheet program such as Microsoft Excel. Generally, spreadsheet data entry requires less set-up time than the creation of a form using a database program. In addition, basic (and sometimes advanced) statistics can be performed with the spreadsheet program.

When all these factors are considered, it is easy to see why we try to use data entry professionals for most of our surveys that require manual entry.

Cleaning the Data File

Before actual data analyses can begin, the tedious task of cleaning the data must be completed. Data cleaning is the process of checking the data to see if they were entered accurately, correcting errors, and rectifying inconsistent responses (e.g., when a respondent's answer to one question indicates that he or she incorrectly completed several items that should have been skipped). Karweit and Meyers (1983) capture the flavor of the data-cleaning task: "Perhaps the most unpleasant aspect of data processing for the survey researcher is the detection and resolution of errors in the survey data" (p. 392). Yet it is something that must be done to avoid the survey data falling prey to the dreaded garbage in, garbage out (GIGO) phenomenon (Alreck & Settle, 1985). It is impossible to obtain accurate statistical results if data are incorrectly entered.

One of our past projects illustrates why data verification is so important. In the days before optical scanning was as cost-effective as it is now, we contracted with external firms for data entry. Two of our specifications are important to note. We required that the data entry be at least 95% accurate; after entering the data from 100 surveys, the contractor had to submit the data file to the survey team so that we could verify the accuracy level. For one project, we found that less than 50% of the responses had been entered correctly.

Types of Data File Cleaning

Two types of data cleaning need to be done. These are examining the accuracy of the information in the data file and checking the consistency of respondents' answers.

▨ *Data Entry Accuracy*

The most obvious data-cleaning procedure is the need to ensure that data were correctly transcribed from the survey form to the data file. If the survey team used a data entry method that does not screen for out-of-range values during input, it can assume that 2% to 4% of the entered data are in error (Karweit & Meyers, 1983). Thus, it is essential that careful data cleaning be performed before data analysis is conducted. This error detection can be done with statistical analyses or verification (Karweit & Meyers, 1983).

The most common method for checking data accuracy uses error detection by statistical analysis (Karweit & Meyers, 1983). Frequencies for each variable are run and out-of-range responses (e.g., a 7 on a 5-point scale) are found. The values for each variable must match those specified in the codebook. For example, if the codebook specifies that the variable GENDER uses only the values 1 (for Male) and 2 (for Female), the survey team should examine all records that have any other values.

The simplest way to identify and subsequently correct incorrect records would be to use a procedure to select all records with values other than 1 or 2 for GENDER. In SPSS-X, for example, the command to select cases with inappropriate values would be SELECT IF (GENDER LT 1) OR (GENDER GT 2). Another procedure, LIST VARIABLES=ID GENDER, could be used to list the identification number(s) for the records selected. The questionable data could be corrected by looking at the original survey and inserting the true value into the data file. This procedure should be repeated for all variables with suspicious values.

The more thorough, but less commonly used, procedure is error detection through key verification. With this procedure, data for each record are examined variable by variable for accuracy. The verification can be accomplished by reentering the data for the total data file or some portion of it and then using computer programs to identify where discrepancies exist between the two data files. Key entry services often have two punchers working on the same data at the same time, with verification occurring throughout the process. Alternatively, one person reads the values from the survey form to another person who compares those values to the information in the data file. Because of the labor intensiveness of this type of data accuracy check, it is usually reserved for small data files or for surveys that require more than the average amount of accuracy.

■ *Response Inconsistencies*

Another potential data file problem involves detecting whether respondents followed instructions. Searching for this type of problem involves determining whether or not respondents correctly followed skip pattern instructions and answered consistently. For this type of data quality analysis, it is advisable to conduct contingency data cleaning (Babbie, 1973). Cross-tabulation (or cross-tab) tables are constructed to determine if the respondents answered consistently or even whether the respondents should have answered a question. For instance, if a cross-tab table shows that a few men answered questions about their most recent pregnancy and maternity leave, the suspect data should be checked against the original survey and corrected within the data file.

Missing Data

It is a truism in the survey business that "the only true solution to the missing data problem is not to have any" (Anderson, Basilevsky, & Hum, 1983, p. 417). Missing data occur despite attempts to eliminate the problem by reminding respondents to answer every question. Given that there is almost always at least one respondent who incorrectly leaves one or more items unanswered, it is important to understand the reasons for missing data before identifying procedures to work around the problem.

Reasons for Missing Data

Some data are missing because the answers are illegible or accidentally omitted. Other respondents skip items that they feel uncomfortable or embarrassed answering (e.g., whether they have been sexually harassed or how they really feel about their boss). Questions that are not fully understood may be skipped. Respondents may fail to answer whole blocks of items if, for example, the items are printed on the back of some of the survey pages, and they do not notice them. Finally, responses to some questions may be omitted because branching instructions are not understood; the result is that whole sections are skipped even though the items should have been answered.

Missing data are a problem more common on paper-and-pencil and scanner surveys than when using a computer. In fact, one of the main arguments for computer administration of surveys is that the computer can generally eliminate most or all missing responses because a response is typically required before the respondent is presented with the next item. In an organizational survey of civil servants' attitudes regarding their retirement system, Doherty and Thomas (1986) found that although about 3% of the responses on a paper version were either missing or completed incorrectly, no responses on a comparable computer version were.

Assessing the Missing Data Problem

The first step in dealing with missing data is to determine how many data are missing—a process that can be made easier if one code (e.g., a period or a space) is consistently assigned as the missing value for all variables during data entry. If the total number of surveys returned is relatively small (less than 100), the actual surveys can be scanned visually for missing data. If the number of surveys is large or the survey is very long, frequency counts should be generated using a statistics program such as SPSS-X, SPSS-PC, or SAS to determine how many missing responses there are and how they are distributed.

For example, on a company diversity survey, 2% of the responses from white male employees were missing, but 15% of the responses from minority employees were omitted. The greater percentage of missing responses from minority employees might be indicative of greater dissatisfaction with the company's diversity programs and policies or greater fear about responding to such sensitive issues. Because the responses are missing, it is impossible to conclude exactly what the data mean. Also, it is somewhat questionable to assume that the results attained from analyzing the nonmissing minority responses are generalizable to the views of the entire sample or population of minority employees. Furthermore, the 15% missing responses among minority employees result in less ability to detect subgroup differences using statistical significance tests (Roth, 1994). As this example shows, the desirable situation is for there to be a low percentage of missing responses, and the missing data to be randomly distributed in the data file rather than clustered in a few cases, subgroups, or survey items.

Handling Missing Data

When most of the missing values can be traced to a small fraction of respondents, the survey team may want to delete these individuals from the data file. Ideally, the candidates for deletion should be compared with the rest of the sample on key demographic variables (e.g., race and gender) to make sure that those with missing data are not systematically different from the rest of the sample. If data are missing on a random basis, there should be no appreciable differences between respondents with and without missing data. On the other hand, if most of the missing values can be traced to a few items, the survey team may want to eliminate these items from the analyses.

We rarely physically delete cases or items. More often, the deletion is done statistically. Rather than delete records, many survey teams prefer to estimate values for the missing responses. They do this with a variety of imputation procedures. The following discussion shows the effects of deletion of cases or the imputation of values.[1]

▓ Listwise and Pairwise Deletion

Listwise (also called *casewise*) *deletion* eliminates all respondents with any amount of missing data from the current set of analyses. In the most extreme case, listwise deletion means that only complete records are included in every statistical analysis conducted (which is the same as physically deleting records with missing values). Listwise deletion might be characterized as the "throwing out the baby with the bath water" approach to dealing with missing data.

The advantage of this extreme form of deletion is that all analyses are performed on the same number of cases. This strategy is only feasible, however, when a small number of respondents have missing data. For example, few people would raise serious objections to dropping 10 or 20 records from a data file that contains several thousand respondents. On the other hand, if a substantial proportion of the sample has missing data on different variables (which often happens), dropping these respondents would not be a recommended solution. Using listwise deletion sacrifices a large amount of good data and may reduce the sample size dramatically. Roth (1994) describes an instance where 10% of the data were randomly missing from a series of five variables. Listwise deletion resulted in the loss of 59% of the cases!

To illustrate further, assume that we have 10 variables and we want to correlate each of those variables with the other 9. If listwise deletion is used, only respondents who have a value for all 10 variables will be analyzed, and each of the correlations in the matrix will be computed on the same number of records. As mentioned above, sample size is reduced dramatically using this procedure.

In contrast, *pairwise deletion* eliminates records based on pairs of variables. When the correlation between variables 1 and 2 is calculated, the only records eliminated are those missing values for variables 1 and/or 2. These eliminated records are reincluded when calculating the correlation between variables 3 and 4, if the records have data for these variables. Compared with a correlation matrix constructed using listwise deletion, a correlation matrix using pairwise deletion usually has a larger number of records. Each correlation in the latter matrix may be based on a different number of records. To justify pairwise deletion, the survey team must assume that values are missing at random.

▧ *Imputation*   Another approach is to fill in the missing responses based on some estimation of what they should be. This process is called *imputation*. Imputation techniques range from simple to quite complex (see Bourque & Clark, 1992; Roth, 1994). A simple technique is *mean substitution,* where the average for the (sub)sample or the population is substituted for the respondent's missing data for that same variable. For example, if an individual has missing data on a satisfaction item, the mean of all other respondents' answers for that item replaces the missing value. If the mean of the sample is 4, then a 4 is substituted for the missing response.[2]

Mean substitution has the advantage of keeping the maximum number of records while holding the sample size constant for all analyses. It works best when missing data are randomly distributed across groups. On the negative side, statistical tests that use average deviations from the mean (e.g., analysis of variance) might be affected if many means are substituted (Roth, 1994). Mean substitution is advisable when less than 10% of the data are missing and correlations between variables are low (Donner, 1982).

Another imputation procedure involves *assigning a neutral value* for the missing response (Babbie, 1973; Roth, 1994). In this technique, the intermediate or neutral response from a rating scale (e.g., 3 on a 5-point Likert scale) is substituted for the missing value. This strategy is probably best used when the respondent leaves out only 1 item in a series (Roth, 1994). For example, it might be useful when a dimension score is determined from the answers to multiple items. In such cases, one substituted (neutral) response should not affect the dimension score very much when it is determined by several items.

A third imputation technique, *assigning a proportionate score to the missing response* (Babbie, 1973), is particularly useful for calculating a multi-item dimension score. For example, a respondent may not have answered one of the six items used to calculate a satisfaction (dimension) score. The respondent's imputed score for the missing response would be the mean of the respondent's own answers to the other items in that dimension. If the respondent's average is 2 for the other five satisfaction items, a 2 will be assigned as the missing response.

We most frequently use the third imputing procedure and prefer to calculate the dimension mean (rather than the sum) of the items. The mean calculation is simpler because a respondent's dimension score is the mean of the completed items. Moreover, software packages such as SPSS allow the user to specify how many valid data points (e.g., valid answers to at least four of the six items) must be present for the mean to be computed.

Our preference also has the advantage of keeping the dimension score on the same scale used for answering the items. In presenting our satisfaction findings, we could, for instance, say white-collar employees with a satisfaction mean of 4.2 (rather than a summed satisfaction score of 25.2) were more positive than blue-collar employees who had a mean of 3.3 (rather than 19.8). The participants in the briefing would know that the mean of 4.2 was between satisfied and very satisfied, whereas a score of 25.2 has no such anchors for interpretation.

▓ *Summary and Caution*   The reviewed methods for handling missing data only hint at the more complicated procedures available (see Roth, 1994, for a review). Once survey teams become comfortable with the discussed methods, they might want to examine the more complex methods. Survey teams and researchers are increasingly using imputation methods because the procedures save much more of the data than when listwise or pairwise deletion is used.

Survey teams that want to examine the interrelationships among variables may find that the imputation techniques do more harm than good. Substituting a number that is based on an arbitrary (but consistent) rule introduces measurement error, and this error can result in spuriously high or low correlations. Therefore, the data should be examined with and without the imputed values to determine whether substituting values for the missing data does more harm than good. After all, the respondent who left some items unanswered did so for a reason. The survey team's imputation may lead to very different answers than those that the respondent would have supplied.

Categorizing and Coding Open-Ended Answers

Open-ended questions, especially those requesting general comments at the end of a survey, are often a good indication of how important survey topics are to respondents. When the survey is very important to respondents, the survey will generate many detailed comments. The rich information that results from open-ended questions must be weighed against the time and labor required to identify response categories and code such data.

Working with open-ended data requires that the survey team develop a system for categorizing and reducing the information to a form that can be collectively examined and summarized. The output from this process can be either a purely descriptive written summary of the results or the assignment of numerical values to different types of responses. This section describes how a survey team might conduct a *content analysis*. Content analysis is a process for coding the narrative answers to open-ended items into a format that allows the responses to be analyzed (Chadwick, Bahr, & Albrecht, 1984; General Accounting Office, 1989).[3] Content analysis generally consists of two tasks: creating categories and content coding.

Creating Categories

■ *Creating Categories for Focused Answers*

The easiest items to content analyze are responses to fill-in-the-blank questions (e.g., "What is your job title?") or multiple-choice items with an "Other (Please specify)" option. A multiple-choice question might ask, "What method of transportation do you use to commute to and from work most (50% or more) of the time?" and supply the following response alternatives: "(1) Drive alone," "(2) Carpool," "(3) Bus/Subway," "(4) Bicycle," "(5) Walk," and "(6) Other (Please specify)." If only a few respondents chose "(6) Other," the survey team may decide to report the percentage of respondents who answered "(6) Other" rather than analyze the responses. If a sizable segment of the respondents chose the "(6) Other" option, the team might conclude that content coding is in order. To code these "Other" responses, the team would start by reading and listing all the

"(6) Other" answers and noting how many respondents gave each response. The resulting list may look like this:

Motorcycle	(7 respondents)
Ferry	(7 respondents)
Train	(3 respondents)
Rollerblade	(2 respondents)

After examining these responses, the team might want to establish some new categories for the "Other" responses (e.g., add "Motorcycle" and "Ferry" categories and assign "Rollerblade" and "Train" responses to a category called "Other Forms of Transportation"). The nature and number of the categories depend on the responses obtained, their frequencies, and the purposes of the survey.

■ *Creating Categories for General Answers*   Open-ended items that assess attitudes (such as items eliciting comments about the survey topics or the quality of the survey itself) are more difficult to categorize and, therefore, are generally not a good mechanism for quantifying attitudes. For example, more than one idea may be expressed in a single answer. A simple approach to the categorization of attitudinal data is to divide comments on a specific topic into positive, negative, and mixed categories and to determine the frequency with which the comments occur in each of these three categories. For example, after categorizing employees' narrative answers about a new performance appraisal system, the survey team might state that 60% of the comments were favorable, 30% were unfavorable, and 10% were mixed. A system like this can be used any time the data contain responses ranging from positive to negative.

A more complex approach attempts to develop mutually exclusive and exhaustive content categories based on the narrative answers. (These two concepts were introduced during the discussion on writing multiple-choice alternatives in Chapter 4.) Survey team members develop content categories for a question's answers by reading a large number of the open-ended responses. As members of the team read the narratives, they write down themes that occur fairly often. These recurring themes serve as the bases for the content categories. It is likely that the responses will have to be read at least twice to develop the initial content categories.

When the tentative set of categories has been developed, the system should be tried on 50 or more randomly selected narrative answers. These answers should not include those that were used to derive the initial categories. The new answers may require revising and adding categories. After a final set of categories has been developed, every response should be coded into one of the categories. This process can be done by assigning a number to each category and writing the number next to the response.

Responses that do not fit into the response categories can be put into a "Miscellaneous" or "Other" category.

Because every response category should be mutually exclusive, what is done when responses fit into multiple categories? In this instance, the survey team needs to decide if responses will be placed in the one, best-fitting category or, responses that contain multiple ideas will be split into different subcategories.

If, in the course of categorization, the survey team realizes that there is going to be an unwieldy number of categories, it should consider combining categories or redefining the categories more broadly. Conversely, if the categories seem too broad to provide useful information (e.g., large, gross categories may mask important differences), the team can either break the existing broad categories into more specific subcategories or start all over redefining the categories more narrowly. It is probably better to start with categories that are too specific rather than too broad. When specific categories are used, the survey team will usually be able to combine categories later if there are too many categories with small numbers of responses. When the data are coded into only a few gross categories, there is no way during the analysis phase to recreate a finer level of detail.

We offer three practical tips when creating categories for open-ended data.

1. At least one knowledgeable person who is not on the survey team should critique the categories early on. An outside party can often see things that team members cannot because they are too close to the problem.

2. Each category should contain a respectable percentage (at least 10%) of the total responses. Choosing 10% as the cutoff is liberal because this cutoff is 10% of the respondents who wrote a narrative answer for the question—not 10% of the people returning the survey. If 30% of the respondents wrote an answer for a given question and 10% of those answers fell into one of the categories, the responses for that category are documenting the answers of 3% ($.30 \times .10 \times 100$) of the total number of respondents.

3. The number of content categories should not exceed 10. This figure is based on Tip 2. If every category has to have at least 10% of the answers (which it will not), it is impossible to have more than 10 categories.

Content Coding

After the team performs the categorizations, it should train at least two other people to perform the coding. A member of the team should code several questionnaires with the coders. Once the coders understand the system, each coder should independently code the same set of answers. A member of the survey team then compares the two sets of codes and discusses discrepancies with the coders. Once the team feels confident that the coders understand the procedure, they can begin coding.

The survey team might want to quantify the quality of the coding. It can do this by calculating the interrater agreement on the set of answers that all coders had to code before being allowed to work on separate sets of answers to a question. *Interrater agreement* describes the degree to which the coders assign narrative information to the same category.

To use this statistic, the coders should be given a single set of comments to code independently. If the coders agree on the categorization of, say, 26 of 50 comments, the survey team will probably find this level of 52% (26/50) interrater agreement unacceptable. Although there are no absolute rules, we recommend that the survey team strive to attain an interrater agreement of at least .80. Anything less may indicate a need to retrain the coders or revise the categories (General Accounting Office, 1989).

Our own approach to open-ended questions has usually been to use these data to complement statistical results from closed-ended items. For example, we sometimes use comments to illustrate a particular point revealed by analyses of the closed items. This strategy lends concreteness and detail to the more abstract statistical findings, making them more vivid and easier for a nontechnical audience to understand.

Survey teams should remember that if they ask open-ended questions, they owe the participants the courtesy of at least looking at responses—no matter how time consuming this task might be. This concern should go into planning the items for all surveys.

Conclusions

The survey team has finished the tedious steps of data coding and entry and file cleaning. All the decisions made about issues such as missing data and coding open-ended responses should be noted in the codebook. A good codebook will come in handy when the survey team later revisits the survey and its findings, as well as during the next survey process phase—data analysis.

Notes

1. The discussion of handling missing values is geared primarily to variables measured on an interval or ratio scale. For items that measure nominal variables such as race or ethnic status or gender, the survey team may wish to assign missing values their own code. For example, the survey team could use 1 for Male, 2 for Female, and blank for Missing. This convention is legitimate because there is no structure in a nominal variable other than that imposed by the coding scheme. This strategy allows other responses from the individuals with missing data on this variable to be used, and the missing data group can be compared with the other groups (such as the gender groups) on all variables of interest.

2. Because the mean response is rarely a whole number, it has to be rounded if only a single column is available to code the missing response. Alternatively, the data file could be reformatted to allow for decimal entries (e.g., 4.2).

3. An alternative approach to the procedure we describe is computer-assisted content analysis using a computer-based text analysis program. These programs count the number

of times a word or phrase appears in a sample of text. To use such software with a paper-and-pencil survey, it is necessary first to enter the open-ended responses into the computer, which may prove very labor intensive. Survey teams interested in this approach to analyzing the answers to open-ended questions should consult Miles and Huberman (1994) and Weitzman and Miles (1995).

Analyzing Data and Interpreting Results

10

The survey data have been entered into the computer and the data file has been cleaned. Now the team is ready for one of the most exciting and challenging survey phases—data analysis and interpretation. The complexity of the analyses depends greatly on who the customers are (e.g., management, hourly workers, human resource professionals), their level of statistical sophistication, and how they want the results presented. Relatively few organizational surveys are aimed at testing a researcher's hypothesis or confirming the validity of a model. Instead, the analyses are typically tailored to identify organizational strengths and weaknesses. Often, the preferred data analysis for organizational surveys is the simplest (Howe & Gaeddert, 1991).

Results from our poll of organizational survey practices in the San Diego area reinforce this last conclusion. When asked to indicate all statistics that were included in reports on survey findings, about two thirds of the respondents indicated that frequencies and cross-tabulations were used. Approximately one-half of the sample reported means and standard deviations. Only around one-quarter of the group said they used statistical significance tests.

Planning the Analyses

Even those who endorse this "simple is better" approach in theory can quickly drown in the computer printouts of an unplanned, unfocused, let's-see-what-will-happen data analysis. For this reason, an analysis plan should be developed before starting the actual data analyses. The plan should specify what statistical procedures will be used on which data so that the survey team runs the data rather than having the data run the team (General Accounting Office, 1993).

Although the task of identifying analyses sounds daunting for even a 50-item questionnaire, many of the pieces of the analysis plan are already in place. For example, subgroups requiring special analyses were probably identified when the survey team conducted focus groups to collect content information (see Chapter 2). Also, the survey team may have combined individual questions into multi-item dimensions (see Chapters 4 and 9) to increase the reliability of the measurements and to make data analysis and interpretation easier. This information can be used for organizing additional analyses. Because the data often reveal unexpected findings, additional statistical procedures may need to be decided after the fact. No one can anticipate every analysis that will need to be performed, but the analysis plan can provide a good starting point.

We recommend organizing the plan around five types of analyses. First, descriptive information is needed for the sample or population. This information includes the response rate and the number or percentage of each category of organizational member (e.g., men/women, managers/hourly workers) who responded. Next, means or percentages based on data from all respondents should be computed for each survey item and dimension. Third, means or percentages should be calculated for selected items and dimensions for key subgroups (such as men and women). Fourth, comparisons between subgroups might be performed to examine if survey responses were similar or different. Finally, if necessary, more sophisticated data analyses should be conducted. Depending on the nature of the survey and the audience that will hear the results, it may be appropriate to compute internal consistency reliabilities for each multi-item survey dimension, to conduct tests to determine if statistically significant differences exist between subgroups of interest, or to calculate statistics (e.g., correlations) to see if responses on two or more variables are related.

The analyses presented in this chapter assume that one or more members of the survey team have some understanding of basic statistics. The chapter is not a statistics tutorial or an analysis cookbook. If the survey team needs a quick review, we recommend refreshers from some of our favorite introductory statistics textbooks (Aron & Aron, 1994; Runyon & Haber, 1991). In a pinch, the organization's technical, computer, and accounting staffs may be able to provide statistical and programming assistance to the survey team. Of course, external consultants can be hired to help with the statistical analyses if sufficient funds are available.

The next section illustrates various types of statistical analyses as they apply to survey data. The data that are discussed are based on the examples used earlier for Organization X (see Chapter 5).

Analyzing the Data

A Review of the Sample and a Description of the Data

Our examples in Chapter 5 illustrated different methods of selecting a sample: random sampling and proportionate and disproportionate stratified sampling. The analyses in this section use a proportionate stratified sample. The same procedures would be followed if everyone in the organization were surveyed (a census) or if a simple random sample was used. A later section describes a disproportionate stratified sample to illustrate post-stratification weighting.

In Chapter 5, we said that a stratified sample is used to ensure adequate representation of subgroups that have particular importance to the issues being surveyed. In proportionate stratified sampling, the same percentage of people is chosen from each subgroup. In our example of proportionate stratified sampling (see Table 5.2), Organization X personnel have been classified according to work site (headquarters and Plants A and B) and organizational level (managers and hourly workers). To guarantee a representative number of personnel in each of the six subgroups, the sample was stratified by the three work sites and two organizational levels.

Organization X administered a short survey measuring satisfaction with one's boss, coworkers, pay, actual work, and overall job to 427 employees. All five of the attitude survey items were answered using a 5-point Likert-response format with options ranging from "Strongly disagree" (1) to "Strongly agree" (5). To keep things simple, for the examples in this chapter we will focus on the analysis of one item: "I am satisfied with my job as a whole."

Describing the Respondents

Table 10.1 shows the number of surveys returned from each group (a total of 354 out of 427) and the percentage of the respondents that each group constituted. In Chapter 11, we recommend that the survey team include a

TABLE 10.1 Distribution of Returned Surveys for Organization X: Proportionate Stratified Sample

Job Type	Headquarters	Plant A	Plant B	Total
Managers				
n	4	21	25	50
%	1%	6%	7%	14%
Hourly Workers				
n	14	124	166	304
%	4%	35%	47%	86%
Total				
N	18	145	191	354
%	5%	41%	54%	100%

TABLE 10.2   Data for Survey Item "I am satisfied with my job as a whole": Proportionate Stratified Sample

	Managers				*Hourly Workers*			
	Headquarters (*n = 4*)	*Plant A* (*n = 21*)	*Plant B* (*n = 25*)	*Total* (*N = 50*)	*Headquarters* (*n = 14*)	*Plant A* (*n = 124*)	*Plant B* (*n = 166*)	*Total* (*N = 304*)
Strongly Agree (5)								
N	—	8	9	17	1	15	0	16
%		38%	36%	34%	7%	12%	0%	5%
Agree (4)								
N	1	10	11	22	2	20	16	38
%	25%	48%	44%	44%	14%	16%	10%	13%
Neutral (3)								
N	3	3	4	10	5	43	75	123
%	75%	14%	16%	20%	36%	35%	45%	41%
Disagree (2)								
N	0	0	0	0	4	31	42	77
%	0%	0%	0%	0%	29%	25%	25%	25%
Strongly Disagree (1)								
N	0	0	1	1	2	15	33	50
%	0%	0%	4%	2%	14%	12%	20%	16%

table similar to 10.1 in its oral or written presentations. Note that the percentage of each subgroup in the sample is equal to the percentage of that subgroup in the population, as shown in Table 5.1 (a feat possible only in the world of made-up examples!).

Frequencies and Percentages

Table 10.2 presents the number and percentage of personnel in each subgroup who gave each possible response on this item. Data are also given for managers as a group and hourly workers as a group. In practice, this descriptive analysis—determining the number and percentages of people who chose each response for each item—is a good way to begin the analysis of organizational survey data (Chadwick et al., 1984).

The analyses for each item in the survey will generate a similar mass of findings. This degree of detail is typically of little use to those who commissioned the survey. They need the findings condensed further. Part of the survey team's job is to examine the findings and weave them into a coherent story.

Most times, the survey sponsors do not need to know what percentage of respondents agreed with the item as opposed to those who strongly agreed. In such cases, response options can be combined to make a table of results that is easier to read and follow. In our example, "Strongly agree" and "Agree" could be collapsed into one category called "Agree," and "Strongly disagree" and "Disagree" could be categorized as "Disagree." To avoid confusion about what agree and disagree mean, the survey team should probably stick with this convention (rather than shifting back and

TABLE 10.3 Responses for Survey Item "I am satisfied with my job as a whole":
Proportionate Stratified Sample

Response	Percentage of Respondents
Agree	26%
Neutral	38%
Disagree	36%

forth between five levels of agreement and disagreement) once it introduces the three levels of responses.[1]

Response percentages can now be presented for three categories (as shown in Table 10.3) instead of five. The survey team loses some of the detail of the findings when using this collapsed technique. This loss of detail makes interpreting the findings much easier, however. Moreover, the smaller number of response options also makes it easier to present the findings (see Chapter 11).

What do the findings tell the survey team? A statement could be made that "Twenty-six percent of the sample are satisfied with their jobs as a whole, 38% neither agree nor disagree with the item, and 36% are dissatisfied."

Some survey practitioners would further condense the information in Table 10.3 into an *agreement index* and report only the percentage of respondents who agreed or strongly agreed that they were satisfied with their job as a whole (Schiemann, 1991). Although an agreement index has the virtue of simplicity, it can also give a distorted view of what the data really show. If a manager was just told that 26% of the sample were satisfied with their jobs as a whole, he or she might assume that most respondents (74%) were dissatisfied. In fact, as this example shows, respondents most frequently indicated that they were neither satisfied nor dissatisfied.

Sometimes data are presented with those who responded "Neutral," "Neither agree nor disagree," or "Don't know" excluded. This *excluding of no opinions approach* (Weisberg & Bowen, 1977) tries to focus the analysis on those who actually expressed an attitude. If the percentages in Table 10.2 are recalculated using this method, we find that 42% of the respondents who expressed an opinion were satisfied with their jobs as a whole and 58% were dissatisfied. This approach may prove useful when there are many "no opinion" responses (which are difficult for managers to interpret) and the goal of the survey results is action oriented—something is to be done based on the findings. To avoid misrepresenting the results, it is a good idea to mention or include as a footnote that the analysis excluded those who responded "Neutral," "No opinion," or "Don't know."

Means and Standard Deviations

A mean (or average) response could also be calculated for each survey item. The mean is simply the sum of the individual responses (e.g., 1 = "Strongly disagree," 2 = "Disagree," etc.) divided by the number of responses. In our example, the higher the mean, the more satisfied the typical respondent is. The average response for this group of respondents is 2.9, slightly below the middle of the scale.

How should this mean be interpreted? When responses are clearly on the agree or the disagree side of the scale (in this example, a value of 4 and higher, or 2 and lower, respectively), results are relatively easy to interpret. In these cases, the survey team can simply state that respondents agreed or disagreed with whatever the survey item addressed. It is rare for average responses to be much above 4 or below 2 on a 5-point scale, however. Thus, an average score of 4 should be interpreted as clear agreement and an average score of 2 should be interpreted as clear disagreement.

If the average response is around the neutral point, interpretation is more difficult. In our example with a mean of 2.9, responses were fairly evenly divided among the alternatives, and the mean response reflects this fact (which is why showing percentages is a good idea in this case). When many or most of the respondents select the neutral point on a survey item, it may mean that they were confused by the question, truly felt neutral on the matter, had no opinion, were ambivalent, or were hesitant to express their true feelings. The survey team may want to conduct postsurvey focus groups or interviews to clarify the meaning of such survey results.

If the findings will later be presented to a statistically sophisticated audience, questions may be asked about the item (or dimension) *standard deviations*. Although the mean is a measure of central tendency that tells about the typical response, the standard deviation is a measure of dispersion or spread that provides information about how far the typical score deviates from the mean (Pilcher, 1990). A small standard deviation means that most respondents' scores fell close to the mean, whereas a large standard deviation means that the scores were more spread out. In our example, the standard deviation was 1.15—a fairly large number for a 5-point scale—indicating that the item responses did not all cluster around the average score. In other words, respondents tended to hold differing rather than consensus views with regard to that item.

Analyzing Subgroup Differences

It is common to break down the survey sample into subgroups to compare responses. When survey teams want to look at the responses of two or more variables at a time, they conduct cross-tabulation (or cross-tab) analyses. If we wanted to know how job satisfaction varied for managers versus hourly workers in each of the three Organization X sites, we could create a 2×3 cross-tab table with worker type (managers, hourly) as the rows and organization site (headquarters, Plant A, Plant B) as the columns of our table. To keep things simple, however, let's compare the job satisfaction of managers with that of hourly workers without regard to organization

TABLE 10.4 Data for Survey Item "I am satisfied with my job as a whole":
Managers Versus Hourly Workers—Proportionate Stratified Sample

	Managers	*Hourly Workers*	*Total*
Agree	78%	18%	26%
Neutral	20%	40%	38%
Disagree	2%	42%	36%

site. Table 10.4 presents the percentages of managers and hourly workers who chose each response category.

Another way of presenting the data would be to calculate means for each subgroup. In our example, the mean response for managers was 4.1, indicating that managers agreed with the statement. The standard deviation for managers was 0.85. On the other hand, hourly workers had a mean response of 2.7—on the negative end of the scale. Their standard deviation was 1.06, indicating that the responses of hourly workers varied more than those of managers.

Managers and hourly workers responded differently to the item "I am satisfied with my job as a whole." How should this difference be interpreted? There are no absolute rules about the interpretation of differences between groups. Schiemann (1991) notes that survey teams may set a criterion of dissatisfaction so that any item for which the negative responses reach a certain predetermined minimal level (e.g., 30%) are flagged for special attention and further analysis. This type of standard could be used for the negative end of any Likert-type scale, not just satisfaction items. Similarly, the survey team could set a practical significance rule that says that any difference of 10 or more percentage points is worth noting. Because managers differed from hourly workers by 10 percentage points or more in their agreement with this item, the team would therefore conclude that managers were more likely than hourly workers to be satisfied with their jobs as a whole.

Other Data Analysis Procedures

■ *General Comments on Statistical Testing*

The survey team could conduct other analyses, including tests of statistical significance. When a significance test is performed, the results indicate how likely it is that the finding (e.g., managers being more satisfied with their jobs than hourly workers) represents a statistically significant difference between the groups, or whether the difference could be due to chance. Typically, we choose the .05 level of probability. If the results attain a probability level of .05 or less, we conclude that the differences are real because such a finding would be expected 5 times in 100 or less if chance alone were operating.

Attaining statistical significance is highly dependent on the sizes of the groups being examined. For instance, if men had a job satisfaction score of 4.2 and the women's score was 3.7, this .5 difference between men and women might be statistically significant if the two groups had samples of 300 each. The same difference would probably not be statistically significant if there were only 10 men and 10 women in each group. As a general rule, avoid displaying, analyzing, or interpreting results for subgroups having fewer than 10 respondents. Statistically, it is not sound practice to use such small samples: Extreme responses by one or two respondents can skew the mean of a small subgroup. Ethical reasons also suggest that subgroups smaller than 10 should not be separately reported because anonymity might be compromised.

Having exceptionally large subgroups can lead to a different type of concern. If two groups each have around 500 survey respondents, very small differences (e.g., a difference of 0.15 on a 5-point Likert scale) between the groups may achieve statistical significance. That is, it is unlikely that the small difference was due to chance, but these small differences may have little practical implications for policy makers.

Interpretation of findings also involves determining whether statistically significant results are meaningful or of practical significance. One way to do this is to look for patterns of differences across related items. Do managers and hourly workers differ in the same direction on the majority of the job satisfaction items? If so, the difference between these two groups is probably not due to chance, and is worth interpreting and reporting. Action-oriented recommendations to management might be merited if the differences are

▨ large enough to be practically significant (e.g., differences of 10 or more percentage points);

▨ fairly consistent across related items; and

▨ statistically significant.

▨ *Testing the Differences in Means of Two or More Subgroups*

Although means and standard deviations are preferred statistics for describing how various subgroups responded to the survey, *t tests* or *analyses of variance (ANOVAs)* can be used to test the difference between groups. A *t* test assesses the significance of the difference in means when only two subgroups are compared. In our example, managers had a mean of 4.08, whereas hourly workers had a mean of 2.66. The computed *t* value is 9. This large value is staatistically significant.

ANOVAs are used to compare means for more than two groups. For example, if the survey team wanted to compare the responses of personnel from the three different organizational sites, a one-way ANOVA would be appropriate. To compare the six combinations of employee type and organization site, a two-way ANOVA would be calculated.

▨ *Testing the Relationship Between Two Variables*

A *chi-square test* is often used to determine if obtained percentages differ across subgroups. The survey team could ask the question "Do managers and hourly workers differ in the frequency with which they agree and disagree with the item?" The percentages listed in Table 10.4 appear to be different, but a chi-square test would be needed to determine if the difference was due to something more than chance. The computed chi square of 83 for this example indicates that the differences are stataistically significant and not likely due to chance.

▨ *Assessing the Reliability of Multi-Item Dimensions*

The type of reliability analysis appropriate for most survey data is called *internal consistency reliability* [also known as *Cronbach's alpha,* 1951]. This method of reliability estimates how consistently the items within a dimension (such as organizational climate) measure the same characteristic. Internal consistency reliability values can range from .00 to 1.00.

The survey team should try to use dimensions that have internal consistency reliabilities of .70 or greater. Usually a dimension's reliability increases as the number of items in that dimension increases. Logically this makes sense. A dimension based on 10 good questions can more reliably measure a characteristic than a dimension which has only one question.

As is true for means and percentages, many of the statistical packages contain programs that calculate internal consistency reliability. Also, some of the programs show what would happen to scale reliability if an item were left out. This type of information is useful when the team needs to delete items from a prior survey to allow more space for assessing new concerns in an upcoming survey.

In preparation for the next administration, steps can be taken (e.g., add more items and reword items that had relatively lower correlations with the other items in the dimension) to increase the reliability of the dimension. Additional information on internal consistency reliability is available in Murphy and Davidshofer (1991).

Poststratification Weighting

When a disproportionate stratified sampling plan is used, *poststratification weighting* procedures may be needed. In Chapter 5, disproportionate sampling strategies were recommended when subgroup analyses are planned, and there is concern that random or proportionate stratified sampling would not guarantee that all subgroups are represented in reasonable numbers. In the proportionate stratified sampling example above, only four people fall into the category of manager at headquarters. Comparison of these four respondents to any other groups would be inappropriate.

Disproportionate stratified sampling ensures that adequate numbers of personnel are obtained in each category of interest. Table 5.3 illustrated a

TABLE 10.5 Distribution of Returned Surveys for Organization X: Disproportionate Stratified Sample

Job Type	Headquarters	Plant A	Plant B	Total
Managers				
n	14	50	56	120
%	4%	14%	16%	34%
Hourly Workers				
n	75	81	78	234
%	21%	23%	22%	66%
Total				
N	89	131	134	354
%	25%	37%	38%	100%

disproportionate sampling scheme for Organization X ($N = 425$), and Table 10.5 shows the distribution of returned surveys ($N = 354$) for that sample. Compared to Table 10.1, there are considerable increases in the numbers of managers and headquarters personnel included in the sample. Conversely, there are corresponding decreases in the numbers of personnel from other subgroups.

Table 10.6 provides data for the item "I am satisfied with my job as a whole" and Table 10.7 shows collapsed percentages. These tables, respectively, parallel Tables 10.2 and 10.3, which were constructed using data from the proportionate stratified sample.

In the disproportionate stratified sample, the highest percentage (40%) of personnel agreed with the statement, and the remaining respondents were almost evenly split between the two other categories of answers. The average response was 3.1—slightly above the middle of the scale.

Table 10.8 shows collapsed percentages for managers and hourly workers. Note that these percentages are close in magnitude to those reported in Table 10.4. Again, the mean response was 4.1 for managers and 2.7 for hourly workers.

The percentages and means for the disproportionate subgroups are almost identical to those for the proportionate sample. (The table was constructed so that the subgroup means from both sampling schemes were approximately equal.)[2] Why, then, was the overall percentage of personnel who agreed with the statement much higher in the disproportionate sample (40%) than in the proportionate sample (26%)?

In the disproportionate stratified sample, managers and headquarters people were overrepresented as compared with the population. Because managers' responses to this item were considerably more favorable than the responses of hourly workers, their increased representation within the disproportionate sample increased overall agreement with the item. It would be misleading to state that, in the population, 40% of the personnel were satisfied with their job as a whole.

TABLE 10.6 Data for Survey Item "I am satisfied with my job as a whole": Disproportionate Stratified Sample

	Managers				Hourly Workers			
	Headquarters (n = 14)	Plant A (n = 50)	Plant B (n = 56)	Total (N = 120)	Headquarters (n = 75)	Plant A (n = 81)	Plant B (n = 78)	Total (N = 234)
Strongly Agree (5)								
N	2	19	19	40	3	10	0	13
%	14%	38%	34%	33%	4%	12%	0%	5%
Agree (4)								
N	4	24	27	55	14	13	8	35
%	29%	48%	48%	46%	19%	16%	10%	15%
Neutral (3)								
N	5	6	8	19	25	28	35	88
%	36%	12%	14%	16%	33%	35%	45%	38%
Disagree (2)								
N	2	1	1	4	19	10	20	59
%	14%	2%	2%	3%	25%	25%	26%	25%
Strongly Disagree (1)								
N	1	0	1	2	14	10	15	39
%	7%	0%	2%	2%	19%	12%	19%	17%

To compensate for subgroup overrepresentation when generalizing from a disproportionate stratified sample to the population, poststratification weighting is commonly performed. This operation makes adjustments for deviations between the way a characteristic is distributed in the sample and its distribution in the population (Henry, 1990). With the use of PC-based spreadsheet programs such as Microsoft EXCEL, the weighting procedure is relatively simple. Each stratum's proportion in the population and its proportion in the sample are determined. The population proportion is divided by the sample proportion to provide weights for the strata. The general rule is that groups that are undersampled compared to their percentages in the population receive weights greater than 1.0, whereas groups whose percentages in the sample are greater than their representations in the population get weights less than 1.0. The new weighted frequencies are totaled and a weighted percentage can be determined. Once the weights are calculated, they can be applied to every analysis.[3]

Two examples will clarify the procedures. Table 5.1 indicates that managers in Plant A make up 6% of the total organization. Yet they are 14% of the disproportionate stratified sample. To calculate the weight for this subgroup, .06 is divided by .14 to obtain a weight of .43. Frequencies for managers in this group are multiplied by .43 to reduce their contribution for the population estimate.

For the second example, hourly workers in Plant B constitute 47% of the population but only 22% of the sample. When .47 is divided by .22, the obtained poststratification weight is 2.13.

TABLE 10.7 Responses for Survey Item "I am satisfied with my job as a whole": Disproportionate Stratified Sample

Response	Percentage of Respondents
Agree	40%
Neutral	30%
Disagree	29%

Note: Percentage of respondents does not total to 100% due to rounding.

TABLE 10.8 Unweighted Data for Survey Item "I am satisfied with my job as a whole": Managers Versus Hourly Workers—Disproportionate Stratified Sample

	Managers	Hourly Workers	Total
Agree	79%	20%	40%
Neutral	16%	38%	30%
Disagree	5%	42%	29%

Note: The last column does not total to 100% due to rounding.

TABLE 10.9 Weighted Data for Survey Item "I am satisfied with my job as a whole": Managers Versus Hourly Workers—Disproportionate Stratified Sample

	Managers	Hourly Workers	Total
Agree	81%	18%	27%
Neutral	15%	40%	37%
Disagree	2%	42%	36%

Table 10.9 presents the weighted percentages for the item "I am satisfied with my job as a whole." Notably, the individual entries do not change substantially when compared to Table 10.8. For example, approximately 80% of managers in the weighted and unweighted groups agreed with the statement. In fact, the percentages of each response type for each subgroup (e.g., managers at headquarters) do not change at all. Only the total (or marginal) percentages are affected by weighting. The weighting has essentially reduced the number of managers so that they contribute less to the

overall percentages. The result of the weighting is that the percentage of agree responses becomes 27% (as opposed to 40% in the unweighted sample).

Interpreting the Results: What Do All the Findings Tell the Organization?

The analyses and some initial interpretations have given the survey team a snapshot of its organization at that time. Now the team begins organizing the findings and answering the general question of how the organization is doing. This section addresses that question by looking at two types of situations. In the more common case, data from only the one survey are available. Less commonly, the survey team has data from the current survey and additional information against which it can judge the organization's current performance level.

Comparing Findings With Other Findings From the Same Survey

Many times, survey teams have to interpret the survey findings as isolated bits of information. This situation occurs when

▪ the items have not been included on a prior survey;

▪ the items have been changed from an earlier administration; and

▪ no information is available on how other organizations perform on the same item(s).

Interpretation of the findings is made all the more difficult because of the type of data that is usually gathered in surveys. Because many survey items assess attitudes, there is no absolute standard for determining how well or how poorly the organization is performing. An organizationwide mean score of 4.1 on a 5-point scale may be viewed as being better than an average of 3.6. But what does an average of 4.1 mean? Is it good or bad? Similar ambiguity occurs when percentages are reported. If 65% of the organization agrees with the item "The annual performance ratings are assigned fairly," how good or bad is this situation? As we mentioned earlier, action-oriented managers will likely find such ambiguity difficult to digest. At minimum, they want something against which they can compare the results.

When faced with interpreting findings from an item or dimension that has been administered only once, a good strategy is to place the finding in context. That is, the survey team should examine the results for the item relative to the results obtained for other items. This process identifies the relative strengths and weaknesses of the organization. If an exit survey measured 15 reasons why people leave the organization, the team might rank the means (or percentages) so that they would be easier to understand. Also, in situations that call for subgroup analyses, the means for each subgroup might be displayed in a column beside the organizationwide findings.

Once the information is arranged in this manner, the survey team determines what the organization is doing well and what it is doing poorly.

Also, it can check whether or not a subgroup's ranking and means (or percentages) are similar to those for the total group and other subgroups. For large organizations, each site, division, or department can compare its own survey results with those obtained for the organization as a whole and with other specific departments or sites. For example, management at Organization X might be interested in comparing the survey results of headquarters personnel with those of the rest of the company. Management finds that the mean for the organizational commitment dimension was 3.1 companywide and 2.7 for headquarters personnel. A closer look at other findings shows that managers at headquarters were above the overall mean in their ratings (4.1), whereas hourly workers were much lower (2.7). Comparing one site's survey results with the overall organization average provides a better framework for interpreting the results than if the results from headquarters are viewed in isolation.

In addition to providing a method for organizing the results, this process of comparing findings with other findings from the same survey helps the team anticipate questions that will arise during the oral and written presentation of findings.

Using Norms: Comparing Survey Findings to Other Standards

A more powerful approach to interpretation would be to compare present survey findings with those for the same items on past surveys within or external to the organization. Such information helps answer management's questions about how the organization is doing relative to where it was in the past or in comparison to other organizations. In both cases, the issue is one of *norms*. Norms are descriptive standards against which decision makers can compare the performance of their organization (Morris & LoVerde, 1993). The survey team may have access to internal norms, external norms, or both.

▓ Internal Norms

Internal norms are developed within an organization and require two or more administrations of an item, dimension, or survey. To use such norms, the survey team compares the current results for an item or a dimension with the results obtained for the same item or dimension on a prior survey. This comparison requires that the items or dimensions be worded exactly the same for all administrations. This is particularly appropriate if the comparison is made using the more reliable multi-item dimension rather than a single survey item.

These types of comparisons allow policymakers to determine whether their organization is performing better than, worse than, or about the same as it did at some prior time. Such information is invaluable to top management. For example, a recent survey of health maintenance organization employees found that in the 2 years since the previous survey, attitudes about salaries and benefits had improved substantially, but attitudes about management had become much more negative. Having norms gives the current data a very useful frame of reference and often helps pinpoint problems before they become pronounced. For example, if satisfaction with working conditions has declined from 80% to 58% in the 2 years since the prior survey, management might conclude that it needs to take corrective actions.

▧ *External Norms*

External norms are standards that reflect how other organizations perform. To prevent misinterpretation of findings, external norms need to use the same item(s) and context (e.g., asking whether sexual harassment has occurred in the past 12 months) on both the current survey and the survey conducted by other organizations. Whenever possible, the survey team should use recent external norms generated for organizations within the same industry (Paul & Bracken, 1995).

If the external norms are old, the survey team may incorrectly compare findings for its organization with another organization's findings obtained under different conditions (e.g., during an economic recession or before downsizing). Similarly, comparison to organizations in other industries could lead to misinterpretations of the survey findings. For example, comparing the tenure of employees in a computer software firm (an industry with very high employee turnover) with that of employees with the U.S. Postal Service (an organization with extremely low turnover) would convince the survey team that its organization was dysfunctional when it may be better off than most organizations in the industry.

Using external norms as the standard for comparison may also give managers a false sense of security. If the organization's survey has a dimension score equal to that of another organization, this level of performance may not be good enough in a work environment where total quality and continuous improvement have become the way to conduct business. It might be more appropriate for organizations to *benchmark*. In benchmarking, the survey team compares its survey results with those for the best organizations rather than simply trying to meet an industrywide average (Morris & LoVerde, 1993). Belonging to a consortia (see Chapter 2) is one method for gaining access to survey information about other organizations and external survey norms.

Conclusion

In this age of rapidly expanding technology, computer software makes it easy to generate a room full of statistical output with the press of a button. More analyses and findings are not always better, especially if they create a can't-see-the-forest-for-the-trees problem. Therefore, the survey team should think, plan, and focus the analyses. The team also needs to have an in-depth understanding of everything it will report. Someone in a later audience may know enough about statistics to ask something that calls the survey team's findings into question. "Don't know" is a fine response on an organizational survey, but it doesn't go over well when an aspiring vice president asks a tough statistical question during a big presentation!

Notes

1. Another reason for collapsing response options is the hesitancy of some respondents to choose extreme responses such as strongly disagree and strongly agree. As Fowler (1995) notes,

> Most analysts divide respondents into two categories, those who agree and those who disagree. The reason for doing this is that there is research that shows that response style may have more to do with people's willingness to choose the extreme response than with differences in the opinions being reported. (p. 66)

2. In a fictional example, such a feat is easy. In real life, however, such perfect representation would be unlikely. If a much lower percentage of individuals in one subgroup (e.g., men) than another group (e.g., women) responded to the survey, follow-up interviews and weighting may be necessary to counteract the influence of the different nonresponse rates.

3. Some statistical programs allow the weights to be applied before analyses are run so that analyses are performed on already weighted data, rather than applying weights to analyses run on unweighted data. The resulting means or percentages will be the same whichever procedure is used.

Presentation of Survey Findings

11

The data have been analyzed and the findings interpreted. Now it is time to present the results. The form this presentation takes depends on factors such as the purpose of the survey, the sensitivity of the results, and the relevant consumers of the survey information. A survey may, for example, be designed to give personnel throughout the entire organization a chance to evaluate their company's cafeteria food and service. In this case, it may be important for survey results to be disseminated quickly and widely. For other surveys, leaders may delay or withhold results, especially if there are indications of a widespread or worsening organizational problem.

The extent of survey feedback is typically determined by organization members other than the survey team. Usually, upper-level management decides the content, form, and recipients of the survey feedback, as well as what follow-up actions will be taken. Although we believe that survey results should be available in some form to the people who took the time to respond, the survey team must understand the constraints it may face when attempting to publicize findings. They can lessen the likelihood of misunderstandings and unrealistic promises about survey feedback and follow-up actions by obtaining upper-level commitment early in the process. Despite such commitment, managers may change their positions when a survey reveals negative aspects of the organization. This problem is particularly a concern when the findings show management in an unfavorable light.

Oral and Written Presentations of the Survey Process

Survey results may be presented in either oral or written form. In some situations, both forms of feedback may be required. Oral presentations primarily highlight information relevant to the audience, often leaving out many of the important but technical aspects of survey development and analysis. For example, personnel at the lower levels of an organization may receive only a brief summary of the results, whereas managers who will be charged with implementing organizational changes based on survey results may require more detailed feedback. Or customized feedback may be prepared so that departments receive only results directly relevant to them. These feedback decisions should be discussed early in the survey process because presenting survey results is time consuming and expensive, especially when customized presentations are required.

Written reports may be technical or not, depending upon the audience for whom they are written. Some written reports may be as simple as an article that appears in the organization's weekly or monthly newsletter. Other written reports might be considerably more technical and comprehensive. In the remainder of this chapter, written reports refer to this more comprehensive documentation. These latter reports document in detail the procedures used to develop and administer the survey. It is usually a mistake for a written report of an organizational survey to read like an academic journal article. The increased technical sophistication in the written report needs to be user friendly and comprehensible enough so that managers can understand and act on the findings.

Regardless of the medium, the key to high-quality feedback is to know your audience! The next section discusses how the survey team can best reach the audience by organizing the presentation with a basic outline.

Organizing the Presentation

To ensure that all aspects were covered in the presentation of survey results, Edwards and Thomas (1993) propose using a simplified version of the American Psychological Association's (1994) guidelines for journal articles. Although this model provides the survey team with a structured format to present a complicated survey in a coherent fashion, the team should realize that it is not presenting a research study to an academic audience. Rather, the format serves only as an outline around which the presentation can be structured. The team must prepare something simple, thorough, and action oriented—three hallmarks of a successful organizational survey presentation.

Most, if not all, of the headings in this section should be addressed in any type of presentation; the level of detail can be adjusted easily. The following discussion focuses primarily on oral presentations but can be adapted for written reports.

Introduction: Why Was the Survey Done?

Although it is important that the introduction set the stage for the findings, the presenter needs to avoid getting bogged down in details during this initial phase. That will mean that relatively little of the presentation time will be devoted to covering the introduction or even the method. The two areas that should be presented in the introduction are the purpose of the survey and background that led to the present survey administration.

▪ *Purpose*

The presentation should begin with a statement of why the survey was undertaken. The purpose statement that was written at the beginning of the survey process can be reused here. When presenting the purpose, the presenter might want to identify the individual(s) most responsible for initiating the survey. This latter step helps establish the context and credibility of the survey and its findings.

▨ *Background* The introduction should also cover the conditions, problems, or questions (e.g., "In the past 12 months, the number of people eating in the company cafeteria decreased by 25%") that led to conducting a survey. If the survey has been administered before, a brief synopsis of relevant results from previous administrations is warranted.

Method: What Was Done and With Whom?

The length of the method section varies greatly depending upon the mode of presentation. A written report should have a very detailed method section. A person should be able to read this part of the written report and replicate everything the survey team did. In an oral presentation, the method section is much less detailed. Most listeners will not need (or want) to hear about survey development in excruciating detail. This information should be available (possibly as back-up slides), however, in case of questions during an oral presentation.

The method section describes the mechanics of survey development and administration. The three major topics that should be covered are questionnaire development, survey administration, and who was surveyed. The order of these topics can be varied to fit the survey team's needs. The key to this section is to make sure the information flows logically.

▨ *Questionnaire Development* The process used by the survey team to create the survey should be discussed. If the questions were developed in-house, the approach to writing and pretesting the items needs to be described briefly. If a commercial survey was used, the presenter should describe the instrument and explain why it was selected.

In an oral presentation, it may help to have copies of the survey available for the audience. The disadvantage of this strategy is that it may give a hostile audience material for criticism (see section below on hostile audiences). Written reports that document the entire survey process should contain a copy of the survey as an appendix.

▨ *Survey Administration* Numerous issues can be addressed in this subsection using very little time or space. The topics that should be covered are

- ▨ the method of survey administration (paper and pencil, computer, or interview);
- ▨ whether the survey was administered in groups or administered to individuals;
- ▨ whether the survey was answered anonymously or confidentially or was identified;
- ▨ how the surveys were distributed and returned (via hand, company mail, U.S. mail, e-mail, etc.); and
- ▨ what follow-up procedures were used to enhance the return of surveys.

▦ *Survey Sample or Population*

The third part of the method presentation is a description of the people who received the survey. If the survey was given to everyone in the organization, the administration is easy to describe. If a sample was chosen, the presenter must tell why a particular sampling method was used and the procedures for selecting the respondents. If stratified sampling was used, this information may be easiest to convey in a table similar to Table 5.2 or Table 5.3.

This is also the point at which the overall number of returned surveys and response rate are presented. For some surveys, it might also be useful to give similar statistics for various subgroups. For example, separate response rates for women and men might be very insightful for a sexual harassment survey. For an organizational climate survey, the response rates might be broken down by department or management level. Furthermore, the implications of a particularly low (or even high) response rate should be discussed. A low response rate needs to be explained because someone in the audience may use this information to challenge the credibility of the results. A high response rate may mean the issue is important to many people or that personnel in the organization feel strongly that the survey has given them a voice.

Results and Discussion: What Did the Survey Reveal?

▦ *Seeing Beyond the Trees to the Forest*

This portion of the oral presentation typically generates the most interest and occasionally the most acrimony. Although a lengthy survey has many results to describe, the survey team should not overwhelm the audience with the details of every finding. Especially in an oral presentation, it is important to choose the most important findings. The best way to identify these findings is to reread the goals and objectives of the survey and to gear the presentation toward answering the original questions. After these questions have been addressed, the survey team can determine which other notable but secondary findings should be presented.

The presentation of findings can be organized in several ways. Two of the more common approaches are presented here. In the first, the findings can follow the same order as the items in the survey. This tactic has the benefit of allowing the audience to see the item or set of items that was used. On the negative side, this approach may not allow sufficient emphasis or time for the central focus of the survey. In the second, the presenter can start with the most central concerns of the survey and progress to important but less central issues as time allows. This strategy has the advantage of focusing on the key topic(s) and reserving as much time as is necessary for the major issues(s) covered in the survey. This approach may not be appropriate for all surveys, especially those for which there are many central concerns or the key topics are not readily apparent.

Within a particular topic, we recommend that the presentation progress from general findings to specific findings. We usually begin with overall statements (e.g., "The majority of personnel favor instituting flex time"), and then provide details (e.g., "Interest in flexible work schedules is especially high among employees with children and with personnel who are taking college or graduate courses on their own time"). This organizing strategy provides the audience with a limited set of general findings on which to hang the details of the results.

▨ *Statistical and Practical Significance*

The sophistication of the presentation of results depends upon the audience. In a written report, tests of statistical significance may be required. In many oral presentations, percentages and means are the most complex statistics provided (e.g., "Close to 70% of those surveyed favored flexible work schedules"). Audience members who know little about statistics may nevertheless repeatedly ask if group differences are statistically significant. At the other extreme are people who want every finding discussed in excruciating complex detail. These two conflicting sets of demands make presenting the findings particularly difficult. It is boring to sit through a presentation that is aimed too low, and it is frustrating to listen to a talk that is complicated beyond one's needs or level of understanding.

Research studies tend to focus on statistical significance, sometimes to the exclusion of the meaningfulness of the findings. On the other hand, findings from organizational surveys are meaningful only if the results are significant and suggest implementable actions. Because organizational survey results can lead to rather dramatic (and expensive) consequences, the consideration of statistical significance should be supplemented with concern for practical significance.

As mentioned in the previous chapter, because statistical significance tests are affected by sample sizes, surveys conducted with samples of several hundred or several thousand respondents may obtain significant results even with group differences as small as .1 or .2 on a 5-point attitude scale. These differences, though statistically significant, may have little practical application in organizations. To avoid jumping to hasty conclusions, the survey team might want to set a practical significance level. For example, in Chapter 10, we suggested that the survey team set some pre-analysis limits for judging which findings are significant. At times, we have used a 10 percentage point difference as a predetermined level of practical significance.

▨ *Just the Facts Versus Findings and Interpretations*

Whether the survey team simply presents the facts or adds interpretation of the findings will depend upon the organization. Some organizations expect the team to interpret the findings and recommend actions, rather than merely report the findings. Underlying this approach is the thought that the survey team probably knows more about the data and findings than anyone else in the organization. At the opposite extreme is the organization whose upper management wants only the raw findings. Upper management itself will then interpret the findings and recommend actions. The team needs to determine the preferred style of its upper management. Incorrect planning in either direction can be disastrous.

Although many listeners are less interested in the numbers than what they mean for the bottom line, some audience members are fascinated with the data. They may make a big deal about group differences in means or percentages that the survey team knows are possibly due to sampling error or random variation and are not statistically significant. Several years ago, one of our colleagues presented the results of an annual personnel survey to top management. To simplify matters, he decided to highlight responses to items that had changed more than 5% between survey administrations and ignore lesser differences that could be due to sampling error. Unfortunately for him, one of the top managers had an engineering background and wanted to know all differences between items, no matter how minuscule. He said to our colleague, "In my business, sir, even a difference of 1 or 2% is important!" It is difficult to explain why two numbers that are somewhat different may not really represent a meaningful difference.

In sum, the keys to presenting and interpreting results are to put the statistics into language that is understandable to the audience, to concentrate on findings that are both statistically and practically significant, and to avoid interpreting the findings beyond what can be reasonably defended. Following these guidelines will give the survey team a firm basis to make conclusions and recommendations.

Conclusions and Recommendations: What Are the Next Steps?

If the organization expects the presentation to include conclusions and recommendations, the team may want to give a short synopsis of the major findings before launching into this final section. The review helps remind the audience of the major findings and establishes a context around which the conclusions and recommendations can be framed.

Although some are hesitant to make recommendations, we view clear, action-oriented recommendations as one of the most important functions for a survey team. We agree with Roberts-Gray (1992) that "data presented without recommendations can frustrate and immobilize rather than facilitate decision making" (p. 177). After all, the team should know more about what the survey findings mean than anyone else in the organization. In making recommendations, however, be careful to base recommendations firmly on the data.

A Hodgepodge of Other Advice

Visual Aids

Oral presentations are typically accompanied by visual aids such as overhead transparencies. For high-level presentations, the quality of presentations can often be enhanced by giving each key player a paper copy of the transparencies. This has two benefits. Attendees can concentrate on what is being said, and there is less likelihood that the audience's notes will contain erroneous information.

Written reports typically contain charts, tables, graphs, and other figures. It is difficult to provide absolute guidelines for such aids because organizations often have standard report formats or ways of conducting presentations. External consultants may have more flexibility in designing their presentations than if a survey is done totally by in-house personnel.

The key point to effective visual aids is to keep them easy to understand. Bullet charts are commonly used to review many sections of the presentation (the introduction, method, conclusions, and recommendations). Like politicians' sound bites on television and radio, bullets should capture major points in very few words. Although it may be difficult to condense major points into one or two lines on a transparency, short bullets are also easier to remember than long, in-depth statements. For this reason, the survey team might want to start each bullet with an action verb (select, assign, administer, etc.).

Data are usually presented in tables or graphs. Most of the time, in an oral presentation, it is best not to mention numbers such as means or percentages without also presenting them visually. The choice of whether to use a table or a graph is an individual one and often depends on the amount of data being presented at one time. It is usually a good idea to use both (not necessarily for the same data); the variety helps maintain audience interest. (In a written report, one or two percentages or means may be listed within a paragraph of text.) Presenting a series of percentages or means or a comparison of groups almost always requires a table or graph. Even when tables are needed to display many numbers simultaneously, the presenter needs to avoid the temptation to include too many numbers in a table—especially when the table is to be projected onto a screen. There are few things more frustrating to the audience than watching a person point to numbers too small to be seen.

Graphs are particularly useful in oral presentations because they can communicate quickly, directly, and entertainingly (Henry, 1992, 1995). Many types of graphs are available. The documentation that accompanies software packages such as Harvard Graphics or Microsoft's Excel provides tips about appropriate graphs for different kinds of data. For example, line graphs are often used to show trends over time (e.g., to determine if job satisfaction has changed over the past 3 years). Bar graphs show the data for discrete groups (e.g., percentages of personnel in marketing, sales, and human resources who attended optional cultural diversity training). Pie charts illustrate parts of a whole and may be used when the responses of a particular group add up to 100% (e.g., percentage of personnel who have positive, negative, and neutral attitudes toward a new training program).

Table 11.1 Example of Presentation Table

Percentages of Managers and Hourly Workers Who Agreed With the Item
"I am Satisfied With My Job as a Whole"

	Managers	Hourly Workers
Headquarters	43%	23%
Plant A	86%	28%
Plant B	82%	10%
Total	79%	20%

There are many variations of the types of graphs mentioned. Professional-looking graphs and tables can be easily produced. With ease of production, however, often comes a tendency to put more in a figure than is needed. For example, three-dimensional graphs with shadows and boxes are visually appealing, but they are often difficult to read. Another caution in graphing is to limit the amount of information presented in a single graph. It is easy to overwhelm the audience and make a figure unreadable or difficult to understand.

Henry (1992) notes that "graphing every bit of data and every possible comparison can have a numbing effect on the interest of the audience; use your judgment about which data are most important and most interesting" (p. 158). One of our colleagues learned this lesson the hard way when she tried to condense the size of a presentation by cramming four complicated bar graphs onto a single transparency. As a result, the audience had a difficult time focusing on what each of the graphs was supposed to indicate.

Table 11.1 and Figure 11.1 present the same data (abstracted from Table 10.6). They show the percentages of managers and hourly workers at the three Organization X sites who agreed with the survey item "I am satisfied with my job as a whole." In this instance, the bar graph (Figure 11.1) does a better job of highlighting the extreme response differences between managers and hourly workers.

When making slides or transparencies, some color enhances presentations. At the same time, too many colors may draw attention away from the content of the presentation and focus attention on visual aids. Use the organization's graphics department to prepare visual aids. The graphics department also will have prepared presentation materials for the same high-level managers that the survey team now needs to impress.

Practice

This advice is particularly relevant for presenters who have little experience in front of an audience or who are not comfortable speaking to groups. Once the initial draft of the visual aids is available, the presenter should

Percentage Agree

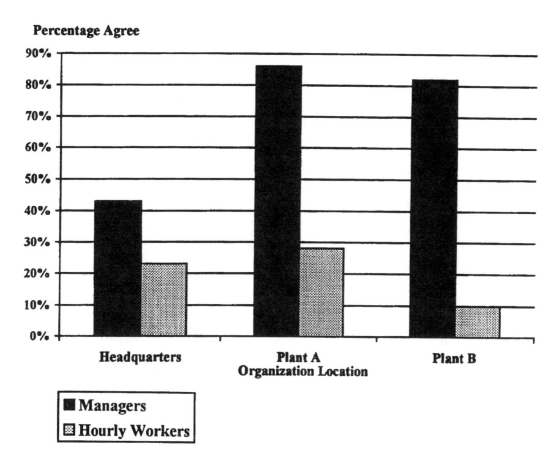

Figure 11.1. Example of Presentation Bar Graph

begin to practice the talk in private. After reaching a level of comfort, the presenter is ready to practice giving the presentation to the survey team (and possibly to people who owe him or her favors). The idea for this second level of practice is to feel at ease talking in front of others, to receive feedback about what is right and wrong about the presentation, and to determine whether the presentation can be made in the allotted time.

If there is a time limit (and there usually is), the presenter should not attempt to have a talk crammed with so much material that it will run past the allotted time. Instead, it is crucial that sufficient time be allowed for the important points (i.e., conclusions and recommendations) that will be made at the end of the presentation. Time for questions from the audience must also be factored into the length of a presentation. With controversial or sensitive topics, even more time should be reserved.

Along the same lines, it may be helpful to prebrief someone in the organizational structure who is close to the highest level of management that will eventually receive the survey feedback. A prebrief may clue the survey team into potential problem spots and also pinpoint information that will be especially interesting to the ultimate audience. This suggestion also holds for written reports.

Organizational politics should be considered before attempting to do a prebrief. If the organization operates in strict hierarchical fashion, appropriate people need to be notified and briefed in the correct order. This consideration is especially pertinent if the survey covered very sensitive material such as racial discrimination or substance abuse. Anyone who has access to the findings before their presentation to the requesting official must be cautioned about maintaining confidentiality.

Handling Questions

At some point, someone will begin asking questions during the presentation or about the report. It is important to handle questions in a professional manner. It is true that the team knows more about the survey process and results than anyone else; it is also possible, however, that the team did not convey what it knew in a clear and understandable way. When asked a question, the presenter should not attempt to dodge it or get hung up on side issues (a tactic favored by many who do not know the answer to the question asked). If the presenter does not know an answer, it is best to say so and offer to find out. The presenter can quickly destroy his or her credibility or that of the survey findings by giving the wrong answer and being caught.

Some presenters prefer to hold all questions until the end of the talk, whereas others want to answer questions as they arise. People often like to ask questions when they first think of them (although frequently if they had waited another 5 minutes, the answer would have been provided). Allowing questions during the presentation has the advantage of taking the heat off the speaker for short periods of time. On the other hand, easily distracted presenters might want all questions to be held to the end. Getting stuck on early issues takes time away from the rest of the presentation. Questions invariably take longer than anticipated. If there are too many questions and the flow of the presentation suffers, the presenter should consider asking the audience to hold questions until later or say that he or she will be happy to discuss a particular question and finding with someone later.

How to Handle Negative News

Because no one likes to take the blame for problems, negative survey information may be coolly received. In the worst cases, management may act defensively, exhibit hostility toward the survey and the survey team, rationalize the bad news, or blame the employees. In such instances, management might view employees as whiners, malingerers, or troublemakers (Wilmot & McClelland, 1990).

To avoid being the messenger who gets shot, it is essential that a balanced approach be used, presenting both positive and negative results. One way to accomplish this difficult objective is to summarize the results in terms of good news-bad news. Presenting some positive information first in the results section can make it easier for management to accept the negative findings that will follow (Roberts-Gray, 1992). In this way, management can get its "warm fuzzies" while the subsequent credibility of bad news is enhanced. Because survey results are rarely either uniformly good or bad, this strategy is not just good public relations. It is an appropriate way to capture a complex set of results.

Another way to handle negative news is to place it in context, especially with the results of surveys conducted in similar organizations (Morris & LoVerde, 1993). A finding that 30% of the women in an organization report being sexually harassed during the past year should set off alarms all the way to the top of the organization. It may help if the presenter notes that other organizations' surveys often find harassment rates of 50% or higher. This comparative information does not mitigate the seriousness of this finding or eliminate the need to address the 30% sexual harassment rate; it just assures management that its organization is not uniquely "bad."

Finally, a way to cushion the blow of bad news is to view the results as a baseline against which future survey results can be compared. This baseline approach is especially useful if the survey is the first of its kind. Findings of high rates of substance abuse, low employee motivation and morale, or poor organizational climate can be described as baseline findings. Future surveys can determine whether things improved after corrective actions were taken.

Handling a Hostile Audience

Members of the survey team may not be privy to all the internal politics surrounding the issues being surveyed. Unfortunately, this fact only may be discovered when the results are presented. For example, a vice president might have wanted to hire an outside consultant to conduct the survey, but his idea was vetoed in favor of allowing employees to form the survey team. During the presentation, the vice president could show his irritation by nit-picking survey items or by questioning the method or results. The presenter lessens the likelihood of losing composure by finding out as much as possible about the important players beforehand.

If someone in the audience gets annoying very quickly, it is a good idea to suggest that comments and questions be held until the end of the presentation. This strategy has several benefits. First, the presentation may go long enough that there is little time for bickering at the end. Second, it is easier to answer questions after the presentation—when the presenter does not have to worry about what comes next. Finally, when only one person is asking all the questions at the end of the presentation, it often becomes apparent that the person has an agenda, and the negative attention is less likely to reflect directly on the survey team.

Linking Survey Results to Action

A survey is not an end in itself. In some ways, it is just the beginning— possibly of a new survey cycle. If the survey is to be a catalyst for change, an essential step is sharing the results with all members of the organization through widespread survey feedback. In one large manufacturing organization, only 11% of those who received feedback felt that the survey results would not be used well, whereas 84% of employees who did not receive survey feedback indicated that the results would not be used well (Management Decision Systems, 1993).

Scarpello and Vandenberg (1991) recommend holding employee feedback sessions with management's approval but without management actually being present. In this way, the survey results can be freely discussed by employees, the underlying meaning of the findings can be explored, and potential ways of dealing with the identified problems can be suggested. In contrast, Johnson (1993) suggests having managers and supervisors lead the feedback sessions to demonstrate their commitment to the survey process. Johnson's suggestion allows management and employees to explore jointly the meaning of the survey results and decide on what actions to take.

In both these approaches, employees are given an active role in interpreting the survey results and suggesting follow-up actions. In essence, employees who raised many of the concerns while completing the survey are empowered to propose solutions to these problems. Active employee involvement brings a major advantage during the period when recommended changes are implemented. These employee-involved changes are more likely to have support throughout the organization than if the changes were suggested by the survey team or dictated from on high (Sahl, 1990).

Hinrichs (1991) recommends a straightforward approach for translating survey results into productive organizational actions, built around feedback of the survey results to organizational members. He suggests that postsurvey feedback sessions be at the lowest level possible so that accountability for change is felt throughout the organization. Hinrichs describes a successful instance where

> each department had access to its own results and comparison benchmarks with the rest of the company. The focus of each meeting was to get specifics out on the table and to brainstorm solutions for their particular situation. Then a process was put into place to be sure feasible suggestions were implemented and appreciation expressed for employees' commitment and involvement. (p. 306)

In addition to employee involvement, the survey team needs management's endorsement of any proposed survey-based changes. To gain the necessary management "buy-in," the team can present the results of the employee feedback sessions to management and help them develop action plans for solving the problems. Rather than being purely informational, feedback sessions can be used in a more constructive fashion. The feedback sessions can lead to discussions that validate, clarify, or qualify the survey results. This input leads to more informed and well-planned recommendations.

In many organizational applications, the best survey recommendations are those that lead to quick and timely actions (Breisch, 1995). To be effective, the recommendations and implemented actions must be followed up. Members of the survey team can serve as part of a follow-up task force (Wilmot & McClelland, 1990). The job of the task force is to record and publicize each of the recommendations, assist in developing clear action plans that hold management accountable, set timetables to enact the changes, develop a tracking system to monitor the progress of implementation, and evaluate the success or failure of the changes (Hinrichs, 1991). One of the best ways to evaluate the success (or failure) of survey-based organizational changes is to do another survey. Sufficient time (e.g., 1 year) must pass before the effect of any organizational changes can be realized. Also, a commitment to do follow-up surveys helps the survey process be viewed as a vehicle for constant improvement rather than as a one-time wonder (Rollins, 1994).

The lack of clear recommendations can hinder efforts to enact meaningful survey-based changes and create cynicism that may hamper future surveys. Rollins (1994) maintains that many organizations do good surveys, but few follow up the results effectively. Futrell (1994) similarly notes that many organizations hire an external consultant to do a survey, read the consultant's report, and then fail to take any action. As we mentioned in Chapter 1, dangers are associated with doing nothing with the results of an organizational survey. Schiemann (1991) accurately points out that

> without a clear process for survey follow-up, one can end up with little improvement, poor communication, management frustration, and disillusioned employees . . . if survey after survey is conducted with no visible action planning, employees will become disenchanted with this process, and future participation and involvement will decline. (pp. 633-635)

While the absence of recommendations can breed cynicism and distrust, bad recommendations can be costly in terms of money, time, and ill will. Although the costs of surveys usually are measured by obvious expenses such as consultant fees, duplicating, and data entry, Scarpello and Vandenberg (1991) insightfully view misguided actions as expensive indirect costs. These authors suggest that incorrect interpretation of findings can lead to organizational actions unrelated to actual problems. At its worst, these unnecessary interventions can create problems where none existed beforehand.

In fairness to management, not all problems identified by surveys can be addressed or solved (Wilmot & McClelland, 1990). Employees may be unhappy with their pay, retirement, or health care plans, but there may not be much that can be done to change these concerns. Therefore, in making recommendations, the team should prioritize the results and stress potential actions and seek solutions that can actually be attained. For instance, providing better training can assuage anxiety over the firm's new computer system; hiring a new food service contractor can resolve a concern for healthy food; and purchasing gym equipment can address dissatisfaction with recreational opportunities.

Conclusions

Preparing and delivering useful survey feedback is one of the most difficult but rewarding tasks facing the survey team. When time and care are put into feedback preparation, the product will be something the survey team can point to with pride. Organizational members can see the fruits of the survey process—perhaps with a new round of activity based on the survey findings.

References

Ajzen, I., & Fishbein, M. (1980). *Understanding attitudes and predicting social behavior.* Englewood Cliffs, NJ: Prentice Hall.

Alreck, P. L., & Settle, R. B. (1985). *The survey research handbook.* Homewood, IL: Richard D. Irwin.

American Psychological Association. (1994). *Publication manual of the American Psychological Association* (4th ed.). Washington, DC: Author.

Anderson, A. B., Basilevsky, A., & Hum, D. P. J. (1983). Measurement: Theory and techniques. In P. H. Rossi, J. D. Wright, & A. B. Anderson (Eds.), *Handbook of survey research* (pp. 231-287). San Diego, CA: Academic.

Armstrong, J. S., & Lusk, E. J. (1987). Return mail in postage surveys: A meta-analysis. *Public Opinion Quarterly, 51,* 233-248.

Aron, A., & Aron, E. N. (1994). *Statistics for psychology.* Englewood Cliffs, NJ: Prentice Hall.

Ayidiya, S. A., & McClendon, M. J. (1990). Response effects in mail surveys. *Public Opinion Quarterly, 54,* 229-247.

Babbie, E. R. (1973). *Survey research methods.* Belmont, CA: Wadsworth.

Barmash, I. (1993, May). Employee attitude surveys: More substance than style. *Across the Board,* pp. 43-45.

Baron, R. A., & Greenberg, J. (1990). *Behavior in organizations: Understanding and managing the human side of work* (3rd ed.). Boston: Allyn & Bacon.

Berdie, D. R., Anderson, J. F., & Niebuhr, M. A. (1986). *Questionnaires: Design and use.* Metuchen, NJ: Scarecrow.

Booth-Kewley, S., Edwards, J. E., & Rosenfeld, P. (1992). Impression management, social desirability, and computer administration of attitude questionnaires: Does the computer make a difference? *Journal of Applied Psychology, 77,* 562-566.

Booth-Kewley, S., Rosenfeld, P., & Edwards, J. E. (1993). Computer-administered surveys in organizational settings: Alternatives, advantages, and applications. In P. Rosenfeld, J. E. Edwards, & M. D. Thomas (Eds.), *Improving organizational surveys: New directions, methods, and applications* (pp. 73-101). Newbury Park, CA: Sage.

Bourque, L. B., & Clark, V. A. (1992). *Processing data: The survey example.* Newbury Park, CA: Sage.

Bradburn, N., & Sudman, S. (1988). *Polls and surveys: Understanding what they tell us.* San Francisco: Jossey-Bass.

Bradburn, N. M., & Sudman, S. (1991). The current status of questionnaire research. In P. B. Groves, L. E. Lyberg, N. A. Mathiowetz, & S. Sudman (Eds.), *Measurement errors in surveys* (pp. 29-40). New York: John Wiley & Sons.

Breisch, R. E. (1995, January). Are you listening? *Quality Progress,* pp. 59-62.

British Telecom. (1984a). *Survey item bank: Volume I—Measures of satisfaction.* Bradford, UK: MCB University Press.

British Telecom. (1984b). *Survey item bank: Volume II—Measures of organization.* Bradford, UK: MCB University Press.

Carney, K. E. (1994, June). Surveys of substance: Communications. *Inc.,* p. 112.

Chadwick, B. A., Bahr, H. M., & Albrecht, S. L. (1984). *Social science research methods.* Englewood Cliffs, NJ: Prentice Hall.

Chun, K. T., Cobb, S., & French, J. R., Jr. (1975). *Measures for psychological assessment: A guide to 3,000 original sources and their applications.* Ann Arbor: University of Michigan, Institute for Social Research, Survey Research Center.

Church, A. H. (1993). Estimating the effect of incentives on mail survey response rates: A meta-analysis. *Public Opinion Quarterly, 57,* 62-79.

Coffey, J. (Ed.). (1993). *Resource manual for customer surveys.* Washington, DC: Office of Management and Budget, Statistical Policy Office.

Converse, J. M., & Presser, S. (1986). *Survey questions: Handcrafting the standardized questionnaire.* Beverly Hills, CA: Sage.

Cronbach, L. J. (1951). Coefficient alpha and the internal structure of tests. *Psychometrika, 16,* 297-334.

Davis, C., & Cowles, M. (1989). Automated psychological testing: Method of administration, need for approval, and measures of anxiety. *Educational and Psychological Testing, 49,* 311-320.

Dentzer, S. (1995, July 17). Anti-union, but not anti-unity. *U.S. News & World Report,* p. 47.

DeVellis, R. F. (1991). *Scale development: Theory and applications.* Newbury Park, CA: Sage.

Dickson, J. P., & MacLachlan, D. L. (1992). Fax surveys? Study finds the time may be right for business research. *Marketing Research: A Magazine of Management & Applications, 4* (3), 26-30.

Dillman, D. A. (1978). *Mail and telephone surveys: The total design method.* New York: John Wiley.

Dillman, D. A. (1985). Mail and other self-administered questionnaires. In P. H. Rossi, J. D. Wright, & A. B. Anderson (Eds.), *Handbook of survey research* (pp. 359-377). San Diego, CA: Academic.

Doherty, L., & Thomas, M. D. (1986). Effects of an automated survey system upon responses. In O. Brown, Jr., & H. W. Hendrick (Eds.), *Human factors in organizational design management—II* (pp. 157-161). North Holland: Elsevier.

Donner, A. (1982). The relativeness of procedures commonly used in multiple regression analysis for dealing with missing values. *American Statistician, 36,* 378-381.

Dunnington, R. A. (1993). New methods and technologies in the organizational survey process. In P. Rosenfeld, J. E. Edwards, & M. D. Thomas (Eds.), *Improving organizational surveys: New directions, methods, and applications* (pp. 102-121). Newbury Park, CA: Sage.

Edwards, J. E., Rosenfeld, P., Booth-Kewley, S., & Thomas, M. D. (1996). Methodological issues on Navy surveys. *Military Psychology, 8,* 309-324.

Edwards, J. E., & Thomas, M. D. (1993). The organizational survey process: General steps and practical considerations. In P. Rosenfeld, J. E. Edwards, & M. D. Thomas (Eds.), *Improving organizational surveys: New directions, methods, and applications* (pp. 3-28). Newbury Park, CA: Sage.

Erdman, H., Klein, M. H., & Greist, J. H. (1983). The reliability of a computer interview for drug use/abuse information. *Behavior Research Methods and Instrumentation, 15,* 66-68.

Fink, A., & Kosecoff, J. (1985). *How to conduct surveys: A step-by-step guide.* Beverly Hills, CA: Sage.

Fowler, F. J., Jr. (1988). *Survey research methods* (1st ed.). Newbury Park, CA: Sage.

Fowler, F. J., Jr. (1993). *Survey research methods* (2nd ed.). Newbury Park, CA: Sage.

Fowler, F. J., Jr. (1995). *Improving survey questions: Design and evaluation.* Thousand Oaks, CA: Sage.

Fowler, F. J., Jr., & Mangione, T. W. (1990). *Standardized survey interviewing: Minimizing interviewer-related error.* Newbury Park, CA: Sage.

Fox, R. J., Crask, M. R., & Kim, J. (1988). Mail survey response rate: A meta-analysis of selected techniques for inducing response. *Public Opinion Quarterly, 52,* 467-491.

Frey J. H. (1989). *Survey research by telephone* (2nd ed.). Newbury Park, CA: Sage.

Frey, J. H., & Fontana, A. (1993). The group interview in social research. In D. L. Morgan (Ed.). *Successful focus groups: Advancing the state of the art* (pp. 20-34). Newbury Park, CA: Sage.

Futrell, D. (1994, April). Ten reasons why surveys fail. *Quality Progress,* pp. 65-69.

Gallup, G. (1988, August). Employee research: From nice to know to need to know. *Personnel Journal,* pp. 42-43.

General Accounting Office. (1989). *Content analysis: A methodology for structuring and analyzing written material* (GAO/PEMD-10.1.3). Washington, DC: Author.

General Accounting Office. (1992). *Using statistical sampling* (GAO/PEMD-10.1.6). Washington, DC: Author.

General Accounting Office. (1993). *Developing and using questionnaires* (GAO/PEMD-10.1.7). Washington, DC: Author.

Giacalone, R. A., & Knouse, S. B. (1993). Identifying security risks in organizations: Development and use of a security exit survey instrument. In P. Rosenfeld, J. E. Edwards, & M. D. Thomas (Eds.), *Improving organizational surveys: New directions, methods, and applications* (pp. 240-256). Newbury Park, CA: Sage.

Giacalone, R. A., & Rosenfeld, P. (1987). Justifications and procedures for implementing institutional review boards in business organizations. *Journal of Business Ethics, 6,* 5-17.

Groves, R. M., & Kahn, R. L. (1979). *Surveys by telephone: A national comparison with personal interviews.* New York: Academic.

Heberlein, T. A., & Baumgartner, R. (1978). Factors affecting response rates of mailed questionnaires: A quantitative analysis of the published literature. *American Sociological Review, 43,* 446-462.

Henry, G. T. (1990). *Practical sampling.* Newbury Park, CA: Sage.

Henry, G. T. (1992). Using graphical displays to empower evaluation audiences. In A. Vaux, M. S. Stockdale, & M. J. Schwerin (Eds.), *Independent consulting for evaluators* (pp. 141-160). Newbury Park, CA: Sage.

Henry, G. T. (1995). *Graphing data: Techniques for display and analysis.* Thousand Oaks, CA: Sage.

Hinrichs, J. R. (1991). Survey data as a catalyst for employee empowerment and organizational effectiveness. In R. J. Niehaus & K. F. Price (Eds.), *Bottom line results from strategic human resource planning* (pp. 301-308). New York: Plenum.

Howe, M. A., & Gaeddert, D. (1991). Customer survey research: Extending the partnership. In J. W. Jones, B. D. Steffy, & D. W. Bray (Eds.), *Applying psychology in business: The handbook for managers and human resource professionals* (pp. 640-652). Lexington, MA: Lexington.

James, J. M., & Bolstein, R. (1990). The effects of monetary incentives and follow-up mailings on the response rate and response quality in mail surveys. *Public Opinion Quarterly, 54,* 346-361.

Johnson, H. J. (1993, July). Training 101: Another look at employee surveys. *Training & Development,* pp. 15-18.

Kagay, M. R., & Elder, J. (1992, August 9). *Numbers are no problem for pollsters: Words are.* New York Times, p. E-5.

Kalton, G. (1983). *Introduction to survey sampling.* Beverly Hills, CA: Sage.

Kalton, G. (1988). Survey sampling. In S. Kotz, N. L. Johnson, & C. B. Read (Eds.), *Encyclopedia of statistical sciences* (Vol. 9, pp. 111-119). New York: John Wiley.

Karweit, N., & Meyers, E. D. (1983). Computers in survey research. In P. H. Rossi, J. D. Wright, & A. B. Anderson (Eds.), *Handbook of survey research* (pp. 379-414). San Diego, CA: Academic.

Kolbert, E. (1992, August 30). Test-marketing a president. *New York Times Magazine,* pp. 18-21, 60, 68, 72.

Kraut, A. I. (1996). (Ed.). *Organizational surveys: Tool for assessment and change.* San Francisco, CA: Jossey-Bass.

Kuhnert, K., & McCauley, D. P. (1996). Applying alternative survey methods. In A. I. Kraut (Ed.), *Organizational surveys: Tools for assessment and change* (pp. 233-254). San Francisco, CA: Jossey-Bass.

Lewin, K. (1947). Frontiers in group dynamics. *Human Relations, 1,* 5-41.

Loftus, E. F., Smith, K. D., Klinger, M. R., & Fiedler, J. (1992). Memory and mismemory for health events. In J. M. Tanur (Ed.), *Questions about questions: Inquiries into the cognitive bases of surveys* (pp. 102-137). New York: Russell Sage Foundation.

Lukin, M. E., Dowd, E. T., Plake, B. S., & Kraft, R. G. (1985). Comparing computerized versus traditional psychological assessment. *Computers in Human Behavior, 1,* 49-58.

Management Decisions Systems, Inc. (1993, Fall). Does survey feedback make a difference? *Decisions Decisions* (newsletter).

Mangione, T. W. (1995). *Mail surveys.* Thousand Oaks, CA: Sage.

Martin, C. L., & Nagao, D. H. (1989). Some effects of computerized interviewing on job applicant responses. *Journal of Applied Psychology, 74,* 72-80.

Matheson, K., & Zanna, M. P. (1988). The impact of computer-mediated communication on self-awareness. *Computers in Human Behavior, 4,* 221-233.

McDowell, I., & Newell, C. (1987). *Measuring health: A guide to rating scales and questionnaires.* New York: Oxford University Press.

Merit Systems Protection Board. (1988). *Sexual harassment in the federal government: An update.* Washington, DC: Government Printing Office.

Merit Systems Protection Board. (1989). *Who is leaving the federal government? An analysis of employee turnover.* Washington, DC: Government Printing Office.

Merit Systems Protection Board. (1990). *Working for America: A federal employee survey.* Washington, DC: Government Printing Office.

Messmer, D. J., & Seymour, D. T. (1982). The effects of branching on item nonresponse. *Public Opinion Quarterly, 46,* 270-277.

Miles, M. B., & Huberman, A. M. (1994). *Qualitative data analysis: An expanded sourcebook.* Thousand Oaks, CA: Sage.

Miller, D. C. (1991). *Handbook for research design and social measurement* (5th ed.). Newbury Park, CA: Sage.

Mitchell, J. L., Weissmuller, J. J., Bennett, W. R., Agee, R. C., Albert, W. G., & Selander, D. M. (1995, May-June). *A field study of the feasibility of computer-assisted occupational surveys: Implications for MPT research and development.* Paper presented at the Ninth Interactional Occupational Analyst Workshop, San Antonio, TX.

Morgan, D. L. (1993). (Ed.). *Successful focus groups: Advancing the state of the art.* Newbury Park, CA: Sage.

Morris, G. W., & LoVerde, M. A. (1993). Consortium surveys. In P. Rosenfeld, J. E. Edwards, & M. D. Thomas (Eds.), *Improving organizational surveys: New directions, methods, and applications* (pp. 122-142). Newbury Park, CA: Sage.

Murphy, K. R., & Davidshofer, C. O. (1991). *Psychological testing: Principles and applications* (2nd ed.). Englewood Cliffs, NJ: Prentice Hall.

Neuman, G. A., Edwards, J. E., & Raju, N. S. (1989). Organizational development interventions: A meta-analysis of their effects on satisfaction and other attitudes. *Personnel Psychology, 42,* 461-489.

Nunnally, J. C. (1967). *Psychometric theory.* New York: McGraw-Hill.

O'Brien, K. (1993). Improving survey questionnaires through focus groups. In D. L. Morgan (Ed.). *Successful focus groups: Advancing the state of the art* (pp. 105-117). Newbury Park, CA: Sage.

Oskamp, S. (1991). *Attitudes and opinions* (2nd ed.). Englewood Cliffs, NJ: Prentice Hall.

Parker, L. (1992, July). Collecting data the e-mail way. *Training & Development,* pp. 52-54.

Parker, S. (1993, September 28). Money talks. *USA Today,* p. B-8.

Paul, K. B., & Bracken, D. W. (1995, January). Everything you always wanted to know about employee surveys. *Training & Development,* pp. 45-49.

Paulhus, D. L. (1991). Measurement and control of response bias. In J. P. Robinson, P. R. Shaver, & L. S. Wrightsman (Eds.), *Measures of personality and social psychological attitudes* (pp. 17-59). San Diego, CA: Academic.

Payne, S. (1951). *The art of asking questions.* Princeton, NJ: Princeton University Press.

Pilcher, D. M. (1990). *Data analysis for the helping professionals: A practical guide.* Newbury Park, CA: Sage.

Rea, L. M., & Parker, R. A. (1992). *Designing and conducting survey research: A comprehensive guide.* San Francisco: Jossey-Bass.

Reeder, L. G., Ramacher, L., & Gorelnik, S. (1976). *Handbook of scales and indices of health behavior.* Pacific Palisades, CA: Goodyear.

Roberts-Gray, C. (1992). Preparing reports and presentations that strengthen the link between research and action. In A. Vaux, M. S. Stockdale, & M. J. Schwerin (Eds.), *Independent consulting for evaluators* (pp. 161-179). Newbury Park, CA: Sage.

Robinson, J. P., Athanasiou, R., & Head, K. B. (1969). *Measures of occupational attitudes and occupational characteristics.* Ann Arbor, MI: University of Michigan, Institute for Social Research.

Robinson, J. P., Shaver, P. R., & Wrightsman, L. S. (Eds.). (1991). *Measures of personality and social psychological attitudes.* San Diego, CA: Academic.

Rollins, T. (1994, Spring). Turning employee survey results into high-impact business improvements. *Employment Relations Today, 21,* 35-44.

Rosenfeld, P., Booth-Kewley, S., Edwards, J. E., & Thomas, M. D. (1996). Responses on computer surveys: Impression management, social desirability, and the big brother syndrome. *Computers in Human Behavior, 12,* 263-274.

Rosenfeld, P., Doherty, L., Vicino, S. M., Kantor, J., & Greaves, J. (1989). Attitude assessment in organizations: Testing three microcomputer-based survey systems. *Journal of General Psychology, 116,* 145-154.

Rosenfeld, P., Edwards, J. E., & Thomas, M. D. (1993). Introduction. In P. Rosenfeld, J. E. Edwards, & M. D. Thomas (Eds.), *Improving organizational surveys: New directions, methods, and applications* (pp. ix-xiv). Newbury Park, CA: Sage.

Rosenfeld, P., Edwards, J. E., & Thomas, M. D. (1995). Surveys (pp. 548-549). In N. Nicholson (Ed.), *Blackwell encyclopedic dictionary of organizational behavior.* Cambridge, MA: Basil Blackwell Publishers.

Ross, S. M. (1992, August). *Computer assisted telephone interviewing technology: Advantages over traditional survey methods for intraorganizational research and policy development.* Paper presented at the annual meeting of the American Psychological Association, Washington, DC.

Rossi, P. H., Wright, J. D., & Anderson, A. B. (1983). Sample surveys: History, current practice, and future prospects. In P. H. Rossi, J. D. Wright, & A. B. Anderson (Eds.), *Handbook of survey research* (pp. 1-20). Orlando, FL: Academic.

Roth, P. L. (1994). Missing data: A conceptual review for applied psychologists. *Personnel Psychology, 47,* 537-560.

Rozensky, R. H., Honor, L. F., Rasinski, K., Tovian, S. M., & Herz, G. I. (1986). Paper-and-pencil versus computer-administered MMPIs: A comparison of patients' attitudes. *Computers in Human Behavior, 2,* 111-116.

Runyon, R. P., & Haber, A. (1991). *Fundamentals of behavioral statistics* (7th ed.). New York: McGraw-Hill.

Saal, F. E., & Knight, P. A. (1988). *Industrial/organizational psychology: Science and practice.* Pacific Grove, CA: Brooks/Cole.

Sahl, R. J. (1990, May). Develop company-specific employee attitude surveys. *Personnel Journal,* pp. 46-48, 50, 51.

Salemme, T. (1995, Jan). Look before you leap! *HR Focus,* p. 7.

Saris, W. (1991). *Computer-assisted interviewing.* Newbury Park, CA: Sage.

Sawtooth Software. (1994). *Ci3 user manual: Version 1.1.* Evanston, IL: Author.

Scarpello, V., & Vandenberg, R. J. (1991). Some issues to consider when surveying employee opinions. In J. W. Jones, B. D. Steffy, & D. W. Bray (Eds.), *Applying psychology in business: The handbook for managers and human resource professionals* (pp. 611-622). Lexington, MA: Lexington Books.

Schiemann, W. A. (1991). Using employee surveys to increase organizational effectiveness. In J. W. Jones, B. D. Steffy, & D. W. Bray (Eds.), *Applying psychology in business: The handbook for managers and human resource professionals* (pp. 623-639). Lexington, MA: Lexington Books.

Schuman, H., & Presser, S. (1981). *Questions and answers in attitude surveys: Experiments on question form, wording, and context.* New York: Academic.

Schwarz, N., & Hippler, H. J. (1991). Response alternatives: The impact of their choice and presentation order. In P. B. Biemer, R. M. Groves, L. E. Lyberg, N. A. Mathiowetz, & S. Sudman (Eds.), *Measurement errors in surveys* (pp. 41-56). New York: John Wiley.

Shaw, M. E., & Wright, J. M. (1967). *Scales for the measurement of attitudes.* New York: McGraw-Hill.

Sheatsley, P. B. (1983). Questionnaire construction and item writing. In P. H. Rossi, J. D. Wright, & A. B. Anderson (Eds.), *Handbook of survey research* (pp. 195-230). San Diego, CA: Academic.

Sieber, J. (1992). *Planning ethically responsible research: A guide for students and internal review boards.* Newbury Park, CA: Sage.

Skinner, H. A., & Allen, B. A. (1983). Does the computer make a difference? Computerized versus face-to-face versus self-report assessment of alcohol, drug and tobacco use. *Journal of Consulting and Clinical Psychology, 51,* 267-275.

Smith, P. C., Kendall, L. M., & Hulin, C. L. (1969). *The measurement of satisfaction in work and retirement.* Chicago: Rand-McNally.

Spector, P. E. (1992). *Summated rating scale construction: An introduction.* Newbury Park, CA: Sage.

SPSS Inc. (1988). *SPSS-X user's guide* (3rd ed.). Chicago: Author.

Stanton, M. (1989). Reporting what we think: The pollsters. *Occupational Outlook Quarterly, 33,* 12-19.

Stewart, D. W., & Shamdasani, P. N. (1990). *Focus groups: Theory and practice.* Newbury Park, CA: Sage.

Tanur, J. M. (Ed.). (1992). *Questions about questions: Inquiries into the cognitive bases of surveys.* New York: Russell Sage Foundation.

Tedeschi, J. T., Lindskold, S., & Rosenfeld, P. (1985). *Introduction to social psychology.* St. Paul, MN: West.

Tuckel, P. S., & Feinberg, B. M. (1991). The answering machine poses many questions for telephone researchers. *Public Opinion Quarterly, 55,* 200-217.

Vazzana, G. S., & Bachmann, D. (1994, Spring). Fax attracts. *Marketing Research: A Magazine of Management and Applications, 6,* 18-25.

Veit, D. T., & Scruggs, T. E. (1986). Can learning disabled students effectively use separate answer sheets? *Perceptual and Motor Skills, 63,* 155-160.

Verheyen, L. G. (1988, August). How to develop an employee attitude survey. *Training & Management Journal,* pp. 72-76.

Weisburg, H. F., & Bowen, B. D. (1977). *An introduction to survey research and data analysis.* San Francisco: Freeman.

Weitzman, E. B., & Miles, M. B. (1995). *Computer programs for qualitative data analysis: A software sourcebook.* Thousand Oaks, CA: Sage.

White House. (1993, September 11). *Setting customer service standards* (Executive Order 12862). Washington, DC: Author.

Wilmot, R. E., & McClelland, V. (1990, May). How to run a reality check. *Training,* 66-72.

Wise, S. L., Plake, B. S., Eastman, L. A., & Novak, C. D. (1987). Introduction and training of students to use separate answer sheets: Effects on standardized test scores. *Psychology in the Schools, 24,* 285-288.

Wollack, S., Goodale, J. G., Wijting, J. P., & Smith, P. C. (1971). Development of the Survey of Work Values. *Journal of Applied Psychology, 55,* 331-338.

Yammarino, F. J., Skinner, S. J., & Childers, T. L. (1991). Understanding mail survey response behavior: A meta-analysis. *Public Opinion Quarterly, 55,* 613-639.

Author Index

Subject Index

About the Authors

Jack E. Edwards is Chief of the Personnel Survey Branch at the Defense Manpower Data Center in Arlington, VA. His prior positions include Personnel Research Psychologist at the Navy Personnel Research and Development Center and Associate Professor of Industrial/Organizational Psychology at the Illinois Institute of Technology. He has examined theoretical and practical concerns in survey methods, personnel selection, performance evaluation, and utility analysis. He also coedited *Improving Organizational Surveys: New Directions, Methods, and Applications* (Sage, 1993). He received a Ph.D. from Ohio University.

Marie D. Thomas is Assistant Professor of Psychology at California State University at San Marcos. Previously she was Research Psychologist with the Navy Personnel Research and Development Center and Associate Professor at the College of Mount St. Vincent in New York City. Her research interests include gender and ethnicity issues and the role of women in the military. She has authored and coauthored numerous publications and coedited *Improving Organizational Surveys: New Directions, Methods, and Applications* (Sage, 1993). She received a Ph.D. from Fordham University.

Paul Rosenfeld is Personnel Research Psychologist at the Navy Personnel Research and Development Center in San Diego and an Adjunct Professor of Psychology at the California School of Professional Psychology. He coauthored two books: *Impression Management in Organizations* (Routledge, 1995) and *Introduction to Social Psychology* (West, 1985) and coedited four other books. He received a Ph.D. from the State University of New York at Albany.

Stephanie Booth-Kewley is Research Psychologist at the Naval Health Research Center in San Diego. Her research interests include personality,

163

survey methodology, and health psychology. She has published articles in *Psychological Bulletin, American Psychologist,* and the *Journal of Applied Psychology.* She received a Ph.D. from the University of California, Riverside.